SOCIOLOGY AND PHILOSOPHY

by
EMILE DURKHEIM

Translated by
D. F. POCOCK

With an Introduction by
J. G. PERISTIANY

THE FREE PRESS
New York   London   Toronto   Sydney   Singapore

The Free Press
A Division of Simon & Schuster Inc.
1230 Avenue of the Americas
New York, N.Y. 10020

A 1974 reprint with additions, published by arrangement with
Routledge & Kegan Paul Ltd.

Library of Congress Catalog Card Number: 74-19680

ISBN Number: 0-02-908580-2

Manufactured in the United States of America

hard cover printing number
1 2 3 4 5 6 7 8 9 10

paperback printing number
5 6 7 8 9 10

CONTENTS

INTRODUCTION
By
J. G. PERISTIANY

THE three papers collected and published together for the first time by Bouglé in 1924 under the title *Sociologie et Philosophie* are discrete in form but integral in subject. Their connecting thread is the dialectic demonstration that a phenomenon, be it a psychological or a sociological one, is relatively independent of its matrix. In this sense they could be styled Essays in Sociological Spiritualism.[1] Durkheim puts forward the thesis that society is a dynamic system and the seat of moral life. It is neither a mechanical robot nor an organism limited by the structure and function of its organs and the possibilities of its environment. Nor is Durkheimian society, as some of his interpreters and *traditori* would have us believe, a system of organs and functions which tends simply to maintain itself against external causes of destruction, like a living organism whose entire existence would be spent in responding in an appropriate manner to external stimuli[2] or to utilitarian needs.[3]

Many of the problems which these papers discuss are present in contemporary thought.[4] It is, perhaps, the sign

[1] The sociological form of 'spiritualism' is the belief that the properties (and interests) of the whole and those of the individuals who compose this whole are not homogeneous.

[2] *Sociologie et Philosophie*, 1924, pp. 132-3 [90-91]. The reference in square brackets is to the present volume. I shall refer to it in future as *SP*.

[3] *SP*, p. 133 [91].

[4] E.g., the relation, in physics, between measurable statistical 'sign' and a non-observable deterministic substratum; the question of the relation between a part and a whole in Gestalt psychology, and that of the independent 'reality' of fixed and interacting objects in Phenomenology.

of a virile mind that it is able not only to invest with an
air of novelty the perennial problems with which it has
come to grips, but to mark them in such a way that its
impress shows clearly through the outworn conceptual
framework. These papers I found invaluable for clarifying
Durkheimian thought at a number of Oxford and Cambridge seminars of which Mr. D. F. Pocock was a most
active member. His lucid translation has overcome many
of the problems which face the translator of Durkheim.
Most of Durkheim's work has now been translated into
English. The publication of the present volume coincides
with an increasing interest in the sociology of values, and
it will be welcomed by those interested in the development
of sociological thought.

If I were asked what I believe to be the basic problems
of Durkheimian sociology and therefore the true guides
to his thought, I would answer: The relation between
Average, Normal and Ideal, and his conception of Creative
Synthesis. The first delimits the subject matter of sociology,
the second provides the main indices to the Durkheimian
social system. The two problems are inseparable. They
arise from a certain conception of the subject; they are
part of the same methodology.

I. AVERAGE, NORMAL AND IDEAL

The question of the relation between Average, Normal
and Ideal is implicitly referred to or directly discussed
in most of Durkheim's work.[1] This is not to say that its
formulation is clear or its terminology consistent. I shall
therefore try to draw the threads together.

The Durkheimian individual is a *homo duplex*, both
I and *We*. This is a polarity, not an antithesis, which is
deeply rooted in his conception of society and of its moving
forces.

[1] See, *i.a.*, Marcel Mauss, *In Memoriam, L'œuvre inédite de Durkheim
et de ses collaborateurs*, Année Sociologique, Nouvelle Serie, I, 1923-4,
pp. 9-10.

Since his earliest writings Durkheim, a student of Wundt and Ribot for a time, showed great deference for psychology when it was confined to its own, that is to the individual, field. But when social phenomena were interpreted in psychological terms as a means to crossing the threshold between the two fields Durkheim rejected this device as methodologically unsound. Whatever the theoretical attitude of the sociologist, the fact remains that the individual is the active agent of culture.[1] What, then, should be the sociologist's attitude towards his behaviour? Should the sociologist study 'dyadic relations' and individual attitudes? Should he construct a mean based on the behaviour of the majority of individuals and then evaluate the normality or the desirability of individual conduct with reference to this mean? To transpose the question: Is the 'social type' coterminous with the conduct of the majority of individuals, and may values and sanctioned social norms be inferred from them? I believe that an answer to some of these questions would not only further our understanding of the subject matter of Durkheimian sociology and throw light on his conception of collective representations, but might also help us to clarify and define our attitude to these problems.

Here it is necessary to proceed with caution and to clear the ground step by step, since Durkheim's terminology and approach have given rise to many misunderstandings concerning his hypostatization of social phenomena.

In his study of suicide Durkheim criticizes Quetelet for explaining the regularity of certain modes of behaviour associated with each society by postulating an 'average man', that is, a personality type characteristic of each society and reproduced by the majority of its individual members. Knowledge of this type is gained by a reversal

---

[1] *Les Règles de la Méthode Sociologique*: 'Apart from individuals there are things which are the integrating elements of society. It is only true that individuals are the sole active elements.' (Intr. to 2nd ed., p. xiv of 8th ed.)

of the process to which is attributed the regularity of the forms of individual behaviour. The personality type is reflected in the mean. Mean and prototype are one.

What, then, is Durkheim's own attitude to the question of social uniformity and of the individual's role in its formation?

In *Règles* Durkheim suggests that a sociological phenomenon may, with regard to its generality, assume two forms.[1] Some are 'general' in the whole extent of the species; they are found, if not in all, at least among the majority of 'individuals'. Variations are confined between two proximate terms.[2] The others are exceptional.[3] Into the composition of the 'average type' enter the characteristics the most frequent in the species under their most frequent form. It should, then, be possible to say that 'the normal type is at one with the average type', and that 'any deviation from this standard of health is morbid'.[4] Here frequency[5] of a certain form of behaviour is equated with normality of this type of behaviour, and what is frequent appears to be not only a standard of normality, but also a standard of health. The statesman himself is advised not to plan for a better—an 'ideal'—future society, but to maintain what is, if this is the general=average=normal= healthy state of society.[6] This is the clinical approach of

[1] *Règles*, p. 69.   [2] *Règles*, p. 69.

[3] 'There are others which are exceptional; not only are they found solely among the minority, but even when they occur they do not endure during the entire lifetime of the individual.' (*Règles*, p. 69.) European societies strongly disapprove of brigandage. In Italy custom is said to be sometimes indulgent to it. 'Such a fact is then abnormal.' (From the introduction to the first edition of *De la Division du Travail Social*, 1893. This forms part of a longer section which was omitted from later editions. I quote from G. Simpson's English translation, p. 432.) Unless otherwise stated further references are to the 6th French edition.

[4] *Règles*, p. 70—'morbid or pathological'.

[5] I use 'frequency' throughout as meaning 'the fact of occurring often or being repeated at short intervals' (*Shorter O.E.D.*).

[6] *Règles*, p. 93. Durkheim nevertheless admits the necessity of shaking off the social yoke, either because under certain conditions

the physician who, in his diagnosis of the state of the organism he is treating, compares the condition of this particular organism to that of the average organism of the same age and sex, using the degree of frequency of that state as his standard of normality and health.

It is at first difficult to distinguish between Durkheim's own method of constructing a standard of normality and the methods at which he levels such virulent criticism,[1] as both seem to use frequency of individual behaviour as their common standard of measurement. The concept with an ambiguous frame of reference is that of 'general'. It may refer either to a single society or to a social type. When Durkheim refers to the characteristics of a social type the units of that type are societies and not persons. If the behaviour of the average individual had been the standard of generality and of social health, then crimes, suicides and acts of self-sacrifice would have been classified together, with respect to their frequency of occurrence, as exceptional and, with respect to 'normality', as morbid and undesirable. But crimes and suicides occur regularly in response to social forces acting within a social system. These qualities of constraint and regularity are among the main characteristics of social facts. They are as characteristic of 'frequent' as of 'sporadic' social phenomena. There is thus no doubt that crimes and suicides are social facts. These social facts are said to be normal and general for a social type when they occur in the average society of that type (considered at a corresponding

'a just contract' is not possible (*Division*, Book III, Ch. 2), or because society is undergoing a process of rapid change and has not yet come to recognize that its value system and its conditions of existence are at variance. The only constraint which may be qualified as normal is the constraint which corresponds to an intellectual or moral, that is a social, superiority. The pressure which is exercised by one individual on another because of superior strength or wealth, 'especially when this wealth does not express his social superiority', is an abnormal one and can only be maintained by violence. (*Règles*, p. 151, note 1.)

[1] Even in *SP*, e.g. p. 121 et seq. [83 et seq.].

stage of its evolution). Thus crimes and suicides, phenomena of rare occurrence in relation to the expectation of behaviour of the average individual within a certain society, are considered as general and normal for the social type to which this society belongs. The characteristic of generality refers to the *occurrence* of a phenomenon within the average society of a certain type, however small the numerical proportion of individuals performing this action within each society of this type. The rate of occurrence is also measured in each society of the type within which the phenomenon occurs, and a certain rate is said to be characteristic of each society of this type, the average rate for societies of this type being normal for this social type. When the term 'general' refers to the relation between a certain phenomenon and a certain society it concerns the frequency of the form, of the character, that the phenomenon assumes in this society. Thus the form of a certain phenomenon may be 'general' for a certain society if that is the form it most frequently assumes within it. The phenomenon itself, in relation to the behaviour of the majority of individuals, may be of relatively infrequent occurrence. A consideration of the characteristics of a number of societies serves to construct a comparative social type. At this, the comparative, level 'general' and 'normal' refer to 'the occurrence of the phenomenon in the average of the societies of this species'. Thus the character of frequency attached to generality refers, at the comparative level, to the number of societies within which the phenomenon occurs, and at the level of a single society to the most frequent form which the phenomenon assumes within that society. I am underlining this point only because it may help us to understand Durkheim's use of terms. For more practical purposes Durkheim's assessment of normality[1] and desirability serves as a link between the two types of frequency.

It remains to be seen why 'general' and 'normal', in

---

[1] '... a social fact can only be qualified as normal or abnormal in relation to a definite social species.' (*Règles*, p. 94.)

their comparative context, have come to be equated with 'desirable'. A phenomenon which is general within a social type is characteristic of the unit within which it is observed. This constant association, this generality, is a manifestation of the regularity with which certain social forces operate within these societies.[1] This judgment (desirability) refers to the relation between a certain phenomenon and the conditions of existence of the social system within which it takes place, and not necessarily to the conformity of an action to a social norm. This existential judgment becomes a utilitarian value judgment when it marks the sociologist's predilection for what is— which includes also the potentialities of what, 'normally', is to be—in preference to the politician's blue-print, when this blue-print originates not in the study of social reality and of the trends inherent in it but in ethical considerations of what, *a priori*, ought to be. If a social phenomenon is general and normal for a social type, one cannot wish for the phenomenon to be other than it is without accepting the responsibility for altering the social system[2] and its conditions of existence. At this level of analysis desirability has a utilitarian connotation.

We may now pass to a more normative and less causal level of analysis, the relation between Mores and Ideals.[3]

[1] *Règles*, p. 36.

[2] In *Règles*, pp. 83-5, Durkheim states his belief (i) that a society without crimes would be abnormal and that the means used to eradicate criminality would be responsible for the creation of new sources of crime; and (ii) that in a society of saints venial sins would assume the gravity of crimes.

[3] Both customs and ideals are moral facts. Durkheim, in a section of the introduction to the first edition of his *Division of Social Labour*, to which I have already referred (see p. x, n. 3), rejects the necessity— or even the possibility—of distinguishing between custom and ideal by using the criterion of gradations in obligatoriness. Even in his famous paper on judgments of value and judgments of reality all important social phenomena (religion, law, economics, aesthetics, morality) are said to be systems of values and therefore ideals (*SP*, p. 141 [96]). Lalande, on the other hand, believes that 'even in moral

Durkheim's genetic and functional approach to this problem and his conception of the contingency of the higher forms of reality temper considerably his analysis of the deterministic relation between statistical sign and social forces.

If one could collect together 'in a kind of abstract individuality the most frequent characters in a species under their most frequent form',[1] one could say that this abstraction constitutes the normal type, and that this normal type is the object of the sociologist's study.

I have assumed in my interpretation that 'most frequent' and 'general' refer, at the comparative level, to the occurrence of a phenomenon in the average society of a certain type, and that the form most frequently assumed by this phenomenon in a particular society of this type is general and characteristic of that society and a sign of the forces which operate within it.

The question, nevertheless, remains whether at a normative rather than at a causal level the student of a particular society would not find it useful to create a standard using the same principles as the comparative sociologist and, transposing normal conduct within the social type with individual conduct within a particular society, construct a model based on the 'average conduct' of the 'average individual'. Should such a model be constructed from this type of data, what would be its degree of 'objectivity'?

This is an early and a basic theme of Durkheimian sociology from its very inception. In one of his first lectures at the University of Bordeaux[2] Durkheim tells his students that sociological conclusions should be reached only after

science there is a part of the ideal which is good without being obligatory.' (See A. Lalande, *Vocabulaire Technique et Critique de la Philosophie*, under 'normatif'. See also his *La Raison et les Normes*, 1948, especially Ch. VIII entitled 'Au delà des normes'.)

[1] *Règles*, p. 70.

[2] *Introduction à la Sociologie de la Famille*, Annales de la Faculté des Lettres de Bordeaux, 1888, to which I shall refer in future as *AFLB*. Durkheim had been appointed the previous year.

sifting a large amount of evidence. He advises them, nevertheless, to be wary of generalizations based solely on the frequency of individual practices. Two of his own examples will, perhaps, render his *caveat* clear.

A traveller observes frequent examples of conjugal devotion and of filial piety. From these field observations he concludes that the family, in this society, is a well integrated unit. Does this constitute a legitimate inference from the observation of the frequency of a certain type of individual behaviour? Durkheim's answer is in the negative, as 'the degree of cohesion attained by the family in a particular society is a state internal and general to the whole extent of society. On the contrary, the events of everyday life on which this kind of observation is based are facts external, transitory and particular.'[1] No doubt they are usually linked to the constitution of the family, but this link is so 'complex' and so 'distant' that the interpretation which joins them together is in danger of being an entirely subjective one.[2] This paradigm implies that it is not possible to gain a sociological, an objective, understanding of social phenomena by simply relating individual practices to average behaviour. An explanation which makes no reference to the accepted norms and values lacks the depth of social perspective. Its very shallowness may lead to a facile subjectivism or ethnocentrism. The generality of a fact, in the sense of the plurality of cases, is significant in this context only in relation to its generality, in the sense of its normativeness. From the observation that most unions are monogynous one cannot infer that polygyny is not permitted, or even that it is not considered as the ideal state.[3] It is the structure of the family, that is

[1] Notice that, in the same way as 'internal' is opposed to 'external', 'general' is opposed to 'transitory' and 'particular'. In view of what follows later 'general' comes to acquire the additional meanings of objective and obligatory—and even of generic.

[2] *AFLB*, p. 265.

[3] Monogyny may be due to reasons which are fortuitous in relation to the system of social beliefs.

the institutionalized and sanctioned modes of conduct referring to its organization, which interests the sociologist. Sanctioned custom[1] is 'what is common and constant in all individual forms of conduct. It expresses exactly the structure of the family or, rather, it *is* that structure. Custom, in relation to the particular incidents of domestic life, is as the generic type of an animal to the detail of phenomena which have the individual organisms as their seat.'[2] Sociology studies norms and not mores. This constitutes one of the cornerstones of Durkheimian sociology. He never departed from it, as is shown by these lines written a few months before his death as an introduction to his unfinished book on 'Morality': '. . . the science of which we outline the plan proposes to reach the moral precepts in their purity and their impersonality. Its object is morality itself, ideal morality poised above individual practices (*planant au dessus des actions humaines*), not the distortions it suffers when it is incarnated in current practices which can only express it in an inaccurate way.'[3] And Durkheim adds in the margin: 'contrast between mores and morals'.[4] Even when individual attitudes tend to conform to the social system of beliefs, as in the expression of public opinion, the sociologist has to refer individual actions to an objective, a normative, model of society, and not to the distorted model constructed from the expressions of public opinion.

This does not mean that individual conduct has no interest for the sociologist,[5] but rather that all its forms—

[1] Durkheim writes, more simply, 'custom'.

[2] *AFLB*, p. 277. Here what is common and general is the 'rule' and not the individual practices, however frequent.

[3] *Introduction à la Morale*, Revue Philosophique de la France et de l'Etranger, 1920, vol. 89, p. 96.

[4] Mauss, note.

[5] However well regulated a function may be, it leaves a large share to individual initiative. (*De la Division du Travail Social*, 6th ed., p. 208.) This latitude of choice is wide for economic phenomena and narrow for religious ones. (*Règles*, p. xxiii, n. i.) In any case, with increasing social

even the most common ones—are a refraction, an ectype, of a model which cannot be reconstituted by piecing them together. Durkheim's advice to the sociologist rings clear and true. It is to study norms and not individual attitudes,[1] social imperatives and not the reaction of the average man to the average man's picture of the social order. For the sociologist it is only in relation to the normative system of beliefs and to the sanctioned channels of action that individual conduct becomes meaningful.

Durkheim was intolerant of the attempt of some individualists to use the individual, seen as a mind and as a sum total of needs, as the key to our understanding of social phenomena. His intolerance of these pseudo-sociologies was one of the reasons for his choice of methods and of terms stressing the norms rather than the practices. It is remarkable that those who accuse Durkheim of 'hypostatizing' social facts seldom seem aware that unless an individual action is referred to a model action, a model action to a system of beliefs and actions, and the system itself to a comparative type of such systems, sociology may be left with the three main alternatives of explaining the part through the part, the part through an inexplicable and often transcendental whole, or of describing without any attempt at explanation.[2] These three approaches,

differentiation the range of individual variations increases. (*Division*, p. 275.) When flagrant individual breaches of morality are not followed by sanctions this is a clear sign that morality is in a state of flux. (*AFLB*, p. 268.)

[1] Without referring them to the norms.

[2] As when the uniqueness of societies is stressed. This approach, which Durkheim associated with historical nominalism, derides the possibility of comparative sociology, *Règles*, p. 94. '... science does not describe the individual but the general.' 'The first task of science is to describe the nature of the things which form its subject matter. But if they are so dissimilar among themselves that they do not form a *genus*, it is not possible to attempt their description by the use of rational means, as in this case each one of them would have to be examined and defined separately from the others. But in each individual thing reside innumerable properties, among which it is not

the psychological and pseudo-functional,[1] the mystical and, finally, the empirical, interesting and valuable as they are in themselves, will, if they are practised to the exclusion of all others, slowly asphyxiate sociology until nothing is left but the name and a jargon whose proliferation will be in direct contrast to the subject's vitality.

The following points have emerged from this discussion:

(1) The frequency of individual repetition of an action is not a sufficient characteristic of a 'social fact'.

(2) The rate of occurrence (whether frequent or infrequent) of a social fact may serve as an index of an underlying social reality and of the trends which pervade it. A scientifically measured statistical rate is a sign of 'a certain state of the collective consciousness'.[2]

(3) A qualification of (1) and (2). The rate of occurrence of a social phenomenon should be measured over a long period of time within one society. It should also be compared with the rate of other societies of the same type. In each society each phenomenon has its own distinctive

possible to choose; how is one to define the infinite? There is, in that case, but one issue: to handle them as do the poets and literary people who describe things as they seem to be, without any rational method.'— Durkheim, 'Quid Secundatus politicae scientiae instituendae contulerit'; thesis, 1892, translated by Alengry in *Revue d'Histoire Politique et Constitutionnelle*, 1937, pp. 405-63. The passage quoted here is from p. 414.

[1] I use the term pseudo-functional to refer to the approach which proffers either biological or psychological explanations of social phenomena or piecemeal explanations of institutions through the inter-relation of their apposite aspects without reference to any whole of which they are parts. This approach is as different from that of Durkheim as behaviourism from Gestalt psychology.

[2] *Règles*, p. 14. Not only do statistical figures 'translate social phenomena in an authentic and objective manner, but they render them in a way which permits the measurement of quantitative variations' (*AFLB*, p. 271). The suicide rate is the product of social factors. When one examines not individual suicides but the rate of suicide, 'this total is not simply a sum of independent units, a collective total, but is itself a new fact *sui generis*, with its own unity, individuality and, consequently, its own nature—a nature, furthermore,

rate of occurrence. The phenomenon is normal when it occurs in the average society of its type.[1] Its rate is normal when it does not vary beyond certain limits associated with the average society of this type.

(4) It is clear that although Durkheim's use of the term 'general' is usually associated with frequency of occurrence, his rapid passage from individual behaviour to a statistical rate, from the universality of the action of a force within a society to a measurement of its effects, and from frequency of the form of a phenomenon within a single society to frequency within a social species, sometimes blurs both the issue and his use of this term. 'General' may thus mean 'generic' and refer to a characteristic quality of a *genus*, in this case of a social type, or it might mean 'frequent'. Lalande[2] rightly notes that this term is so ambiguous that it is best, whenever possible, to replace it by a more precise one. The term 'normal' is equally ambiguous. It may refer either to the majority of cases or events of a certain type, or to 'what constitutes the average or the mode of a measurable character'.[3] It also indicates a relation with a norm.

Thus statistical analysis permits both the disjunction of the general from the individual in each society and, at the same time, the measurement of certain social forces as reflected in the rate of occurrence of social phenomena. The phenomena and the rate of their occurrence are healthy and normal when they reflect conditions of existence which are associated with the average society of this type. But there is also another kind of social imperative and another meaning to 'normal'. This is associated

dominantly social' (*Suicide*, trans. by J. Spaulding and G. Simpson, p. 46). Durkheim is careful to add that between sign and the underlying reality it represents there is always some discrepancy.

[1] Considered at a corresponding stage of evolution.

[2] For a very illuminating discussion of these points see A. Lalande, *Vocabulaire Technique et Critique de la Philosophie*, Société Française de Philosophie, 5th ed., 1947, under 'général' and under 'normal'.

[3] Lalande, 1947, under 'normal'.

with conformity, not with social forces *in toto* but with sanctioned norms of conduct. Statistics reflect the degree of conformity with these norms, and Durkheim considers 'demography' as a valuable adjunct to the sociology of the family.[1] On the other hand it is not possible to arrive at the norm from a statistical analysis of the behaviour of the majority of individual members of society. Thus neither the normality nor the normativeness of a mode of conduct—nor its desirability at either level—may be assessed with reference to majority behaviour. If the majority of individuals do not commit crimes, this does not mean that crimes are abnormal; neither does it mean that a crimeless society is desirable (or, indeed, possible). Passing from the level of social forces to that of social norms, if the majority of citizens evade their fiscal duties this does not mean that fiscal regulations do not exist, or that it is not desirable that they should be sanctioned. A certain phenomenon is normal for a certain type (at a comparable stage of evolution) when the phenomenon occurs in the average society of this type. Thus it appears that average, normal and healthy (which, in this context, means 'desirable') coincide at the level of the social forces and of conditions of existence. On the other hand the relations between social ideals and actual behaviour are of an entirely different order.

II. Autonomy and Creative Synthesis

The hiatus is clearly indicated by Durkheim's teacher and friend, Emile Boutroux, in a course of lectures delivered at the Sorbonne in 1892-3.[2] 'In order to introduce sociology into the concert of sciences it would be necessary to consider social facts only under their mechanical equivalents. Thus, the physicist considers physical agents

[1] *AFLB*, p. 271.
[2] 'De l'Idée de Loi Naturelle dans la Science et la Philosophie Contemporaines'. I am quoting from the 'Nouvelle Edition', 1950.

only under their measurable manifestations. But do these equivalents, already so difficult to find in psychology, exist in sociology? It is believed that statistics will provide them. But is it not necessary constantly to complement statistics by using judgment? When is one in the presence of numbers which lend themselves to only one kind of interpretation and which express immediately the social reality to which they refer? Does the number of people who know how to read and write provide a faithful measure of the development of instruction in a country? Could the religious movement be measured by [figures relating to] the trade in ritual objects? It happens that, in this domain, men of tact and experience, through the use of literary expressions and without the use of figures arrive at a truth that no mathematical quantification is capable of attaining. If, one day, social facts are reduced (ramenés) to physical facts this, in effect, would mean that an infinite number of intermediaries has been inserted between the two, intermediaries whose very existence we do not suspect at the present moment.'[1]

It is clear that Durkheim's own methodological position is equidistant from that section of the historical school whose ideal is the descriptive monograph, and from those philosophers who believe on the one hand that single societies 'are contingent and transient combinations without independent reality',[2] and on the other assert, like Comte, that the proper unit of study is humanity. Durkheim is opposed to both empiricism and mysticism, two ways of thinking which are very closely connected.[3] He rejects 'theological and idealist metaphysics' which derive the part from the whole, as well as individualistic sociology which explains the whole through the parts.[4] It is for this

[1] Boutroux, op. cit., p. 132.
[2] 'sans realité propre' (Règles, p. 94).
[3] SP, p. 97 [67]; Règles, p. 42.
[4] SP, p. 41 [29]; 'Only the universal is rational. The particular and the concrete baffle understanding' (Division, p. 275).

last reason that he also rejects materialistic interpretations of social phenomena. Durkheim does not hold that
social facts *are* material things, but that they should be
approached as if they had a reality independent of that
of the observer. He considers himself to be a 'rationalist',
as he believes that it is possible to discover causal relations
in social conduct, and he defines his own position as
'spiritualist' in that he explains the whole through properties which are characteristic of the whole.[1] It is to this
approach that I shall now turn.

A social system presents the individual with institutionalized channels and models of action. It provides him with
'collective representations', that is with a conceptual
framework of action.

It would be easier, perhaps, to understand Durkheim's
conception of a collective representation through his
description of an individual representation. Durkheim
criticizes Huxley, Maudsley and James for reducing
consciousness to the level of an epiphenomenon of the
organism.[2] According to Durkheim the formation of mental
images is to some extent dependent on the structure,
not only of the nervous system itself, but of the mind.[3]
The more abstract the concept, the larger the number of
non-organic factors which will have to be taken into
consideration. When these abstract representations, that
is ideas, have come into being, new associations are
constantly formed between them, and this constant
synthesis follows principles which are but partially
dependent on the organic matrix of the mind. Images
combine to form ideas and ideas become part of a complex
system of concepts. The higher the level of synthesis, the
more distant from the organic substratum, the smaller the

[1] *Règles*, pp. vii-viii.
[2] *SP*, 'Individual and Collective Representations'.
[3] 'All representations on coming into being affect, apart from the
organs, the mind itself, that is to say, they affect the present and
past representations which constitute the mind . . .' *SP*, p. 24 [17].

degree of its immediate organic dependence and the higher the degree of social influence.

Durkheim, of course, is fully aware that it is individuals who think and not a monstrous Group Mind. What he wishes to suggest is that the pattern, the grammar of thought, of a certain society is connected with its historical development and with the structure of society and of its system of values, which is something other than the structure and development of individual minds.

But even here I may be going much further in a materialistic direction than Durkheim would have wished an interpreter of his thought to go.

To understand social facts Durkheim advises us, *inter alia*, to ask two types of question: (i) How have things come to be what they are? and (ii) What is their position in the social system? He advises us, that is, to ask both an historical and a sociological question, and he divides the sociological question into two parts—a functional, that is a dynamic, question and a structural, or static, one.

If we apply this method to social modes of thought, we shall have to ask the following three questions which Durkheim considers equally relevant to a sociological analysis: What is the historical development of these modes of thought, what is their function, what is their structural relation to their social system?

Let us use one of his own examples. If we are concerned with understanding the Greek Pantheon, we shall have to retrace its historical evolution and to relate this evolution to variations of the social structure such as the way in which the patriarchal family was organized and the gradual fusion of clans into the *polis*.

When we have answered these questions our understanding of the Greek Pantheon will certainly be deeper than when we began our analysis, but we shall also find that the constitution of the pantheon does not reflect any specific aspect of social morphology. Once certain ideas concerning the gods have come into being—ideas which are a *sui generis* reflection of the social system—these ideas become part of a system of ideas with its own internal consistency and, like language, with its own laws of development. There is no doubt that economic and political conditions will affect the development of ideas concerning this Pantheon, but these ideas are as free in relation to particular elements in the structure as the individual representations in relation to nervous cells.

Thus autonomy is a concomitant of synthesis and the degree of autonomy is a function of social complexity. The more highly differentiated is a society, the less its system of ideas tends to reflect any specific element of the social system. Nothing could be more foreign to Durkheim, after his first attempt at a mechanical explanation, than a materialistic interpretation of history, which he formally rejected.[1]

This is especially true of his treatment of ideals.

The core of the social system, its very soul, says Durkheim, is the system of ideals of value,[2] to which is related a social hierarchy of values. In the same way as we distinguish in Durkheimian sociology between the sacred and the profane, a methodological distinction is drawn between a judgment of value and a judgment of reality.

A judgment of reality is a judgment of existence, as when I state that a certain object has weight. It also expresses the partiality a person has to an object, as when I express a preference for wine. A judgment of value

[1] Durkheim considers historical materialism as another type of epiphenomenalism: see his review of Labriola's *Essais sur la conception materialiste de l'histoire* in R.P., XLIV, pp. 645-51; also a recent article by A. Cuvillier under the title 'Durkheim and Marx' in *Cahiers Internationaux de Sociologie*, 1948, vol. iv, pp. 75-97.

[2] The problem of value was introduced into the stream of nineteenth-century French philosophical thought chiefly by sociologists, of whom Durkheim was the most prominent, under the form of the relation between judgments of value and judgments of reality. See L. Lavelle, *Traité des Valeurs*, vol. i, 1951, pp. 134-6 and 525-8.

expresses a relation between a socially held ideal and an object. It is neither a statement concerning the nature of things nor a subjective appreciation, but a social, an objective, evaluation. 'This is an heroic action' is a judgment of value. Objects become sacred and judgments attribute value when they reflect a social ideal.[1]

What is an ideal, and what is its relation to the other parts of the social system?

Society may go through three different phases according to the intensity of its social life. On some rare occasions —and Durkheim quotes among his examples the great Christian crisis, the Reformation, the Renaissance and the French Revolution—certain events 'due to diverse circumstances'[2] activate the rhythm of social life. The intensity of social life takes the form of constant private and public meetings between its members. The greater the intensity of social life, the greater the probability that out of this crucible of ideas some new ideal will emerge, an ideal which will act as a catalyst of emotion and as a purified[3] reflection of this unique historical moment. In this ideal individual members of society will commune. When individuals commune in an ideal which transcends their egoistical and sectional interests, these interests are provisionally set aside. It is when individuals set aside their egoistical interests, that is their profaneness, and identify themselves with the supreme, that is the sacred, aims of society, that reality appears to be at one with the unattainable ideal and the kingdom of God and that of Caesar appear to merge on the same plane.

These rare occasions, which Durkheim calls 'creative periods', are evanescent. Soon sectional interests reassert themselves and the new ideal survives only as a memory. This memory, nevertheless, is precious to society as it

---

[1] As the 'ideal' is, in its own way, 'real' there is no difference of nature between judgments of value and judgments of reality.

[2] *SP*, p. 134 [91].

[3] From subjective refractions and egoistical interests.

reminds its members of a period of supreme integration. Anamnestic rites are therefore held which re-enact the birth of the ideal. This, for Durkheim, is the main function of religious and civic ceremonies.

It is in relation to these ideals which reflect the supreme moments of social synthesis, of creativeness and of oneness, that is measured the value of social actions.

Each society, says Durkheim, has its own system of ideals, and the type of man which every society holds up as ideal provides the key to the entire social system and is the reason of its unity.[1] What is the relation, we may then ask, between the ideal archetypes of action and the social system?

If by social system we mean, as Durkheim does here, the total social reality then, by definition, the ideal is included in it. We are also told that a certain ideal type corresponds to a social system—but not that it reflects it accurately. What the ideal reflects is both a functional interdependence and a polarity. An ideal, like a religious symbol, reflects both the actual state of society and its aspirations. The aspirations perform a normative function and the actual state of society provides the necessary conditions for the realization of these aspirations. This is the supreme creative synthesis. Ideals are links between the past, the present and the future, and enjoy not only a large measure of relative autonomy from their morphological substratum, but also provide society both with its identity and, being unattainable, with its dynamic drive.

What, then, is the relation between average individual practices and ideals? I have already tried to show that a standard constructed from the behaviour of the 'average individual' may in no way correspond to the social norms which are highly valued by society, and to which individual conduct is expected to conform. Also that mere frequency of a form of conduct does not endow it with the characteristics of constraint and objectivity which are

[1] *SP*, p. 82 [57].

among the main attributes of social facts. 'Between "I like this" and a "certain number of us like this" there is no essential difference.'[1] Two examples may serve to illustrate this methodological attitude.

The first is taken from *Le Suicide*. 'In moments of national emergency', says Durkheim, it is a social axiom that the interests of the collectivity transcend those of its individual members, but if one examines 'la moyenne des individus' one will discover but a very small flame of self sacrifice.[2]

If we turn to the normal type itself we find[3] that during periods of transition the normal type does not correspond to the actual state of one or more societies of this type, but to a state which has already been superseded. It then becomes extremely difficult to evaluate behaviour. Socrates, for example, was a criminal if judged by his attitude to the 'normal type' and he was, thus, rightly put to death. But if he were judged with reference to the new ideal, which reflected more or less accurately the trends of the emerging social system, Socrates died the death of a martyr and of a true prophet. Thus, not only may ideals bear but little relation to actual practices, but their dynamism is such that they may be in advance of—and therefore at variance with—the norms of conduct upheld by courts of law.

What a sociologist studies, says Durkheim, is not the social forces themselves but the external signs through which they become manifest. I have tried to show that the different levels of synthesis correspond to different depths of social reality, the lower level being the matrix and the higher the phenomenon which is partly autonomous and partly interdependent with its matrix. At first Durkheim believed that the social realities which lent themselves to mensuration reflected accurately the more complex social forces. In *Division of Labour* Durkheim attempts to

---

[1] *SP*, p. 122 [83].   [2] *Le Suicide*, pp. 356-7.
[3] *Règles*, pp. 75-6; *SP*, pp. 93-4 [64-5].

show that 'signs' such as the density of population, the number and the speed of means of communication, are visible symbols of social solidarity. It is therefore possible to study the sign as an accurate representation of the social force with which it is related.[1] A year had gone by when Durkheim wrote in *Règles:* 'We have made the mistake in our *Division of Labour* of overstressing material density as the accurate expression of dynamic density.'[2]

This discussion concerning the relative independence of the different levels of synthesis opens the way to two conclusions which throw some light on Durkheim's methodological position. The first concerns his use of the term 'function' and the second the nature of society.

First, function; Durkheimian society does not balance, 'as in a budget', ends achieved with energy spent. Its standard of value is not that of the happiness of the greater number or of the average citizen. It is not social utility or even the survival of society under its material form. In the final analysis society is a system of ideas with which society is so completely identified that it would disappear rather than forsake the Ideas[3] which it incarnates. In what is, perhaps, his most significant single paper entitled 'Judgments of Value and Judgments of Reality', read at the International Congress of Philosophy held at Bologna in 1911,[4] Durkheim declares that to explain the function of ideals by the contribution they make to the maintenance of the equilibrium, the solidarity or the survival of a society (as some sociologists tend to do, in the mistaken belief that they are following Durkheim's teaching), is to

---

[1] *Division,* p. 241. It is also true that in *Division* itself Durkheim points to a number of exceptions (Ch. III), and that he stresses that it is not necessary to discover whether increase in one type of density *causes* an increase in the other, but that it is sufficient to treat them as concomitant variations. (*Division,* p. 238.)

[2] *Règles,* p. 140, note 1.

[3] When Durkheim writes Idea he wishes to denote that he is using this term in its Platonic sense.

[4] *SP,* pp. 117-42 [80-97].

misconstrue the central tenet of his sociology, which assumes that, in social life, not only are all individuals subordinated to society, but that society itself is a system of ideas, a system which is neither an epiphenomenon of social morphology nor an organ devised to satisfy material needs. Even when individuals change their social environment they cling to the ideals of their society of origin as to the main symbols of their social identity. This point is well borne out by recent studies of ethnic minorities in the United States.

Thus it appears that the different parts of the social system: the demography, the material culture, the non-institutionalized modes of thought and action, the institutional structure and the system of values, enjoy a certain degree of autonomy in relation to each other, and that the function of a social organ may vary while the form of the organ remains constant.[1] It is, therefore, difficult for a sociologist to discover simple causal relations, to make accurate predictions, or to initiate and plan social change. Durkheim advises the sociologist to establish a classification of social types, to trace concomitant variations between various phenomena such as the division of labour and the type of segmentation, social solidarity and suicide or crime. Finally, structural and functional analyses are necessary in order to understand the relation of a part to a whole. Durkheim is careful to add that stress on the structural approach seems more profitable in the study of primitive peoples, as in highly differentiated societies, that is, in societies with a high degree of synthesis and flexibility, the relation between organ and function,[1] and between Ideas and social morphology, is a tenuous one. A systematic analysis of the conceptual framework of society, a study of 'les lois de l'idéation collective', which is as yet in its infancy, is essential to the development of sociology. Durkheim envisages the study

[1] 'Cours de Science Sociale: Leçon d'Ouverture', *Revue Internationale de l'Enseignement*, XV, 1888, pp. 43-4.

of systems of beliefs as forming a new branch of the subject.

The second point which arises from this analysis of his idea of creative synthesis concerns the nature of society. Durkheimian society provides the framework and the recognized channels of action. Public opinion uses a social scale of values in order to evaluate both ends and means. The very categories of thought and the language used to communicate them have a social framework. Society is, thus, not only the structural, the static, matrix of action but it also exercises a normative, a dynamic, influence on every step of its development. It is, in a way, both the ends and the means. Religion itself is a system of symbols through which society takes cognizance of itself,[1] and God is the concept of totality, that is of the most abstract form of the concept of society.[2]

Nevertheless this introduction would miss its mark if it failed to convince that the Durkheimian individual is not a puppet in the hands of a robot society. Society limits the possibilities of action—it does not determine each individual action. It provides through differentiation,[3] creative synthesis and the birth of ideals a scale of values, and therefore a choice between various possibilities. The less egoistical the choice, the higher the value. The supreme values and religion are intimately associated.[4]

Durkheim believes that even his treatment of the relation between statistical 'signs' and social forces operating in certain social contexts (e.g. increase in the number of suicides with increasing old age, and therefore with increasing non-attachment) does not affect the issue of

---

[1] *Suicide*, p. 352.   [2] *Formes Elementaires*, p. 630.

[3] The conception of 'man' gradually transplaces that of member of a particular society. ' . . . the more general the common conscience becomes the more it makes room for individual variations.' *Division*, p. 275.

[4] Cf. A. Comte's 'la fatale solidarité de la morale et de la théologie'. The recognition of this 'solidarity' is one of the reasons for Durkheim's mundane explanation of religious phenomena.

free will, although he considers this question as being a metaphysical one. If the causes of the uniformity of social phenomena had been vested not in external social forces but in man himself, the particular person who was the carrier of these forces would have been unable to escape their effect. When, on the other hand, these forces act in such a manner as to determine a relatively uniform number of suicides in a particular age-grade, they do not determine which particular individual within this age-grade has to commit suicide.[1] The synthesis partially liberates social life from the limitations imposed on it by the characteristics of its constituent parts.[2] It also liberates the parts so that the same institution may fulfil various functions without having to undergo a structural realignment.[3] Synthesis not only liberates the individual from too close a social tutelage, but it liberates the organ from the function, the effect from the cause, and the world of ideas from the more material aspects of its morphology. We may say that creation liberates the creator from the creature as well as the creature from the creator—if creator and creature are seen as complementary notions whose full meaning can only be understood when they are seen in relation to each other. With respect to these problems Durkheim's sociology marks a definite evolution in relation to the conceptions of Saint-Simon and Comte. The new science, according to Comte, studied society as a complex whole whose elements are linked by bonds independent of their organic substratum. With Durkheim some of these bonds

---

[1] *Suicide*, p. 368, note 1.

[2] Durkheim, of course, does not believe that social systems are formed of a number of disparate elements artificially brought together before they are integrated in a synthesis. Each part reflects the whole—but it only reflects it partially. One of the reasons for this lack both of complete integration and of complete passiveness is that each part may preserve characteristics due to a past state of its historical development (e.g. some characteristics of the prohibition of incest related to the type of social system within which the prohibition arose).

[3] *SP*, p. 42 [30].

3

become partially free of the institutional structure itself.[1] Saint-Simon and Comte created pseudo-religions when they sensed that a social system cannot endure without a hard core of unquestionable values. Durkheim's solution was to make the existing social Ideals contingent[2] with respect to, and incommensurable with, either egoistical interests or utilitarian social needs. The solution—on the sociological plane—is an honest one. It permits the inclusion of all human phenomena in our field of study, but it does not aim at the knowledge of ultimate truths—a knowledge which is both outside our field and beyond sociological means of investigation.

[1] Bréhier, *Histoire de la Philosophie*, II, 4.
[2] Contingent='not determined by necessity'. In French it is not used in the sense of 'conditional'.

TRANSLATOR'S NOTE

DURKHEIM has suffered much at the hands of would-be admirers, but the fault does not lie entirely with those who have ascribed to him certain notions which, in fact, he did not hold. Although for the most part he is a careful writer, he is liable to be carried away on occasion by metaphor, and even in those parts of the present work which were not intended for oral delivery he is from time to time given to rhetoric, and this especially where the genders of French nouns encourage a certain anthropomorphism. The translator's work is essentially interpretative, and in order to render Durkheim's thought accurately I have frequently found it necessary to translate the same French word variously as it occurs and according to context; similarly, one word in English often serves to translate two distinct French words. Such things are inevitable since the correspondence between words in the two languages is rarely an identity of meaning. We must presume, however, that Durkheim chose his words deliberately, and the reader is therefore advised to refer, in those passages which appear to him to be most significant, to the original French in order to see what words Durkheim actually used.

Where it seems profitable I have expanded Durkheim's notes and supplied references which may be of interest. I have tacitly corrected several misleading misprints which occur in the two French editions.

I should like to express my great gratitude to Dr. Peristiany for his discussions on the various problems which arose and for his painstaking revision of the English text.

D. F. P.

PREFACE TO THE ORIGINAL EDITION

WE have collected and now publish some essays by Emile Durkheim which appeared recently in the *Revue de Metaphysique et de Morale* and in the *Bulletin de la Société française de Philosophie*. They all have one thing in common in that they throw light upon Durkheim's thought, not only about this or that particular sociological problem but also about the general problems that ordinarily occupy philosophers—the relation of spirit to matter, conscience and nature, reason and sensibility. They show in what way and to what extent sociology revives philosophy. Since sociology is coming nowadays to take a larger place in the curriculum of our schools and Ecoles Normales, it seemed to us that this collection might be of some service and be found to fill a present need by suggesting the orientation and themes of discussion.

Durkheim, in order to continue the work of Auguste Comte, found it necessary to specialize and to limit the field of his studies. Sociology cannot progress unless, as in all sciences, the number not only of objective but also of specific researches is increased. Comte, caught up by a grandiose ambition, talked freely of humanity in general. He did not ask himself whether it might not be necessary to distinguish different types of society and different forms of evolution, but embraced in his bold syntheses all categories of social facts. His followers must be more modest. In order to advance the science each one must bind himself to a particular series of problems.

Submitting himself to this discipline, Durkheim concentrated his attention upon moral problems. From the *Division of Social Labour* to the *Elementary Forms of Religious Life*, and including his *Suicide*, his chief preoccupation remained that of explaining the essence of morality, the role that it plays in societies, and the way that it grows and develops there in expressing the ideals (*aspirations*) of those societies. These studies all relate more or less directly to the sociology of morals. Let us remember that for him they were not to remain simply theoretical. His greatest ambition was to arrive at practical conclusions which should bear fruit in social action. To arrive at this point there was for him no other road than that of positive science. One can see in the discussion on the *Determination of Moral Facts*, as in the introduction to the *Division of Labour*, the care that Durkheim constantly exercised to avoid mysticism, in which the human reason might founder, to refute by the fruits of his research those who claimed that in matters of morality science had failed, and to offer a foundation for conscience itself in facts established by positive observations. We may affirm that in this sense Durkheim's desire was to speak, even in matters of morality, the language of a specialized scientist, not that of the philosopher.

Chiefly because sociology had to prove its right to existence, not only by positive researches but also by discussion of principles, he was led into treating in this way great general and ever-present problems. It is rare that a science in its infancy is not obliged to philosophize in order to obtain a foothold; it achieves its individuality by limiting its field. It sets the mind reflecting upon the relations of science to science, the differences of method, and the hierarchy of forms of being: all questions which imply a philosophy.

Furthermore, as Durkheim developed his researches, he saw that they not only led to a better understanding of the role and the value of this or that particular moral rule or discipline but also to a new conception of the relations of mind, and even reason, with nature. An explanation of the dualism which is the particular characteristic of human kind began to take shape in his mind. Durkheim was not content to leave half-glimpsed the general conclusions to which he was moving, and thus was born what is nowadays often called 'sociologism': a philosophical attempt, that is, to crown the objective, comparative and specialized studies of sociologists with a theory of the human spirit.

*   *   *   *   *

The articles which we publish here will perhaps help to resolve a certain number of ambiguities to which the tendencies of this sociologism have been prone. It will be seen very clearly, in particular, how it is distinguished from materialism, organicism and social utilitarianism, with which there have been several attempts to confuse it.

People have allowed themselves to be deceived by certain prominent maxims from the *Rules of Sociological Method*, taken out of their contexts. When Durkheim tells us to treat social facts 'as things', it is to help us free ourselves of prejudice and to warn us that we must not rely upon ourselves and consult our own feelings when we seek to establish the essence, origins and functions of the different human institutions; it was not an attempt to reduce their laws of development to those of matter, nor to explain the interior by the exterior, the superior by the inferior. On the contrary, Durkheim was one of those who insisted most upon the fact that society is 'above all a composition of ideas'. As he himself says, sociology should direct its attention not only to the material forms but also to the mental states; it is a study of moral climate. By their moral consciences men are bound together. Collective beliefs are the vital knot of the whole society.

There is no doubt that in his earlier works Durkheim took pleasure in insisting upon the close relationship that appeared between the beliefs and the actual form of their social milieu. According as the size of groups, the density and mobility of the component individuals vary, the relation between the collective and the individual minds varies and the beliefs which the former sanctify become less effective and finish by giving place to the cult of individualism. Thus 'social morphology' helps us to understand this process of evolution. Once formed, collective representations combine, attract and repel each other according to their own particular psychological laws. Durkheim is very concerned to point out that men's religious ideas, and all the more their scientific notions, are very far from being simple reflections of the social forms themselves. He was thus very far from wishing to impose upon sociology explanations of a materialistic tendency.

The very early article published here, *Individual and Collective Representations*, brings out clearly this anti-materialist tendency, and should suffice to save certain critics from gross misunderstanding of his thought. We do not know of any more vigorous refutation of atomism in psychology. Durkheim demonstrated peremptorily the absurdity of attaching ideas to cells. For him the existence of the memory is sufficient to establish that the life of representations cannot be inherent in neural matter; as it has its own way of being, so it exists by virtue of its own forces. For the reactions of the cerebral elements upon each other are received and represented by the memory, not individually but as a whole in what we might call their communal existence. Wherever there is communal life, there are effects that pass beyond the properties of the particular elements; the synthesis is creative. This is why, in the same way that the knowledge of what happens in the cerebral cells will not give us the key to individual representations, the knowledge of what passes in the individual mind does not give us the key to collective representations; here as there we have to reckon with what the whole adds to the parts.

We believe that here we have touched upon a central point in Durkheim's philosophy. In the same way that for Tarde the ruling idea was that of biological contagion—beliefs and desires passing from mind to mind like microbes from organism to organism—so for Durkheim the governing idea was that of the chemical synthesis which produces effects that the properties of the constituent elements would not lead one to expect. Durkheim, discussing the charges of materialism which had so lightly been levelled at him, pointed out that he had learned from Renouvier the lesson that the whole is more than the sum of its parts. He could well have added that his most direct predecessor, Comte himself, had never tried to explain the superior by the inferior. In spite of the distortions of many interpretations there was no monism in positivism. It recognised that at each new order of being new forms appear which are to be studied in their originality by special methods suited to them. Chemistry no more gives us the key to biology than biology does to sociology. On this point the philosophy of Auguste Comte is very close—despite all that in other respects separates them—to that of Émile Boutroux, who was Durkheim's master at the Ecole Normale. These two influences converged to make him realise what he called 'the contingence of higher forms of reality'. He is ready to demand for collective life that relative autonomy which is necessary and sufficient to preserve the rights of the soul.

* * * * *

If Durkheim refused to deny the originality of mental life in the realm of theoretical philosophy, so much the more did he stress its value in the field of practical philosophy. This conviction is at the root of his constant opposition to purely utilitarian tendencies in morality, as also to the limitations with which he charged the organicist theory.

When Durkheim says that 'morality begins in the membership of a group', and when he is seen to subordinate personal to social duties and demonstrate finally that today the primary duty of man is to carry out his professional duties, several people concluded that his doctrine tended to reduce individuals to the role of organs and that he saw moral rules as above all maintaining the cohesion, persistence and life of the great organisms which are social beings.

The thought of Durkheim is higher and much more complex. This is most clearly seen in his lecture to the congress at Bologna which contains his penetrating remarks upon the origin of *Judgments of Value*. The authority with which they are clothed, the way in which they impose themselves and their tendency to strive for universality are in his eyes a sufficient proof that they expressed something quite different from the actual properties of things or personal subjective preferences. In the realm of aesthetics as of economics, religion and morality, the imperatives that establish the hierarchies of things and of people are pre-eminently expressions of collective will. Will it be said that they aim only at assuring the cohesion of the group so that it can the better maintain its life? The life which they maintain is not an ordinary kind of life, but a spiritual life which in fact, as Auguste Comte said, helps the principle of humanity to predominate over animality in the lives of the members of the society.

Durkheim put it himself with admirable brevity: 'Society is not a system of organs and functions . . . it is the centre of a moral life (*le foyer d'une vie morale*)'. He points out also that it is to underrate society if one sees it only as a body organized to perform certain vital functions. 'Its true function is to create the ideal.' Thus it constitutes an original centre through which nature passes in order to surpass itself.

From this point of view society does not appear only to exert pressure, but is also a means of elevation to the individual. He profits by the disciplines that the exigencies of the communal life impose. To borrow and alter the image of Kant, without this atmosphere the soul could not spread its wings, would be unable to fly. This is a liberating dependence. In the early chapters of *The Division of Labour* Durkheim refused to agree that the value of a moral rule, like that of professional duty, lies in the degree to which it promotes the advancement of civilization. But it is apparent from the examples he gives that there he understands by civilization the increase of material goods. He refused to measure morality by even these collective utilities. It is a different matter if one understands by civilization the whole assembly of spiritual goods which are at once the instrument of individual perfection and of social communion. Here Durkheim would agree that society has for function the maintenance of civilization; its essential role is to make possible, in preparing the conditions of spiritual life, the realization of humanity.

* * * * *

These brief remarks should suffice to show how far the philosophy of Durkheim takes us from the materialist and organicist philosophies with which it has been likened. Thus understood, Durkheimian sociologism will be seen far more as an effort to found and justify in a new manner the tendencies of spiritualism.

C. BOUGLÉ.

THE LIFE AND WORK OF
EMILE DURKHEIM

By
Talcott Parsons

EMILE Durkheim (1858–1917) may be called one of the two principal founders of the modern phase of sociological theory, the other being his somewhat younger contemporary Max Weber. In his four major works, starting with *The Division of Labor in Society* of 1893 and ending with *The Elementary Forms of the Religious Life* of 1912, and in a large number of articles, monographs, and carefully worked out courses of lectures (several of which have been published posthumously), Durkheim established a broad framework for the analysis of social systems that has remained central to sociology and a number of related disciplines, particularly anthropology, ever since. Even those who basically disagree with it take it as a major point of reference. This frame of analysis underwent substantial development in the course of Durkheim's own career, but it focused continually on the nature of the social system and the relation of that system to the personality of the individual.

Durkheim was born in the town of Epinal in the Vosges, not far from Strasbourg. He was of Jewish parentage, and some of his forebears were rabbis. Indeed he was expected to be a rabbi himself until he became an agnostic. He

Source: "Émile Durkheim," pp. 311–320 in Volume 4 of *International Encyclopedia of the Social Sciences*, D. L. Sills, ed. (New York: Macmillan Publishing Co., Inc. and The Free Press, 1968). Copyright © 1968 by Crowell Collier and Macmillan, Inc. Reprinted as amended by permission of publisher and author. Bibliographical emendations copyright © 1974 by the publisher.

attended the famous École Normale Supérieure in Paris, together with such luminaries as Henri Bergson, Jean Jaurès, and Pierre Janet. His primary focus was on philosophy, but he already had the strong concern with political and social applications that he retained throughout his life. He was too rebellious to rank high among the *agrégés* of his year, and his first academic appointments were as teacher of philosophy in several provincial *lycées*.

In 1885–1886 Durkheim took a year's leave of absence to study in Germany, where he was particularly impressed by the work of the psychologist Wilhelm Wundt. A professorship of sociology (combined with education), the first in France, was created for him in 1887 at Bordeaux, and he remained there until, in 1902, he realized the ambition of all French academics; he was called to a professorship in sociology and education at the Sorbonne in Paris. There he gathered round himself a distinguished group of younger men, including Henri Berr, Marcel Granet, François Simiand, Maurice Halbwachs, and, not least, his own nephew, Marcel Mauss. In the most intimate relationship to his own work, Durkheim founded and edited the very important journal, *L'année sociologique*. On two significant occasions he became very much involved in political affairs: during the Dreyfus case and during World War 1. And over a considerable period he was actively concerned with applied sociology, most notably perhaps in the field of education.

The first three of Durkheim's four books, the *Division of Labor*, the *Rules of Sociological Method*, and *Suicide*, were all published during his Bordeaux period, in 1893, 1895, and 1897 respectively. Then there was an interval of 15 years before the *Elementary Forms* (1912) appeared. After the move to Paris, Durkheim was deeply involved both with his teaching and with the group discussions and activities centering on *L'année sociologique*. It is clear, however, that his thought was developing very rapidly and continuously during this period: witness such fundamentally important articles as "The Determination of Moral Facts" (1906) and "Primitive Classification" (Durkheim & Mauss 1903). The great book on religion, then, was the ripe harvest of a long process of intensive cultivation.

There is evidence that the war was a very great blow and strain to Durkheim. Not only was the cost to France high indeed: Peyre tells us (1960) that over half the class that entered the École Normale in 1913 was killed before the war ended; but Durkheim also lost his only son in 1916. These strains may well have helped to cause his own death from a heart attack, on November 15, 1917, at the age of 59.

Intellectual background. Despite some controversy about the influence of his stay in Germany, the evidence shows that Durkheim's thought was rooted overwhelmingly in French intellectual history. In the remoter background, Descartes and Rousseau were the most important, although in quite different ways. Much closer to him were Saint-Simon, Auguste Comte, and his own teacher, Fustel de Coulanges, as well as such others as Émile Boutroux.

Durkheim's deep concern with the prominent contemporary intellectual currents of other countries, especially England and Germany, was authentically French: it is no disparagement of the originality of French thought on problems of man and society to say that it filled a mediating position between the two wings of the main European trends of thought, British empiricism and utilitarianism and German idealism. In a crucial sense, modern sociology is a product of the synthesis of elements that have figured most prominently in these two traditions, and it seems to have been the mediating character of his French background that gave Durkheim a distinctive "place to stand," from which he contributed so effectively to this synthesis. Hence a brief sketch of both "wings" will help in the understanding of Durkheim's own orientation and statement of problems (see also Parsons 1937; 1965).

As both these traditions developed, perhaps the crucial problem was what happened as the Cartesian approach to the problem of knowledge was adapted to the analysis of *action*. The British position is clearest in the economic branch of utilitarian thought, although it dates from the earliest utilitarian formulation by Hobbes: man is conceived as having not only "sensations" or "ideas," in the epistemological sense of Locke, but also what the economists called "wants" (and what Hobbes, speaking in a political context, went so far as to call "passions"). The wants define the goals of action, whereas knowledge of the situation in which action takes place provides guidance for the instrumental use of resources (including the individual's own capacities) toward the satisfaction of these wants. Mere knowledge of the situation clearly does not suffice to satisfy wants; the situation must be changed in desired ways and prevented from changing in undesirable ways. Throughout, the point of reference is the conception of an individual acting in pursuit of his own "interests."

This frame of reference provided the background for a most important development in the analysis of action, namely, a first technical analysis of the structuring of social means for the satisfaction of wants. The economists, by considering how a plurality of individuals, as producers and consumers, interact in the division of labor and exchange, ingeniously extended Hobbes's formulation—of men interdependent in their interest in "power"—to a conception of *social systems of action* coordinated by the market and the monetary mechanism rather than of action by discrete individuals. As far as it went in classical economics, this conceptual venture was brilliantly successful; but its exceedingly limited scope gradually became evident in two borderline contexts.

One concerned the analysis of the bases of action of the individual. The inadequacy of classical economics here lay not only in its tendency to assume "wants" as given but also in its lack of a clear-cut way of establishing relationships among the different wants of a single individual, to say nothing of the different wants of several persons interacting in the same social system. Without concepts to establish these relationships, the treatment of wants as given easily shaded over into the assumption of their randomness. Likewise, shaky assumptions were made with respect to the problem of "rationality," that is, of the relation between means and wants conceived as ends. In this context, the empiricist–utilitarian tradition tended to a reductionism that is still very much with us; it moves from consideration of the characteristics of the social system (in the economic case, a market system) to the consideration of the properties of constituent units (i.e., individuals rationally engaged in want-satisfaction), then to the wants, next to the psychological determinants of the wants, and eventually to their biological conditions.

The second problematic context bordering on classical economic analysis concerned what we now call the problem or order. How could the relational structure of a market economy be expected to have even a minimum level of stability when the individual participants were in the first instance bound to that structure only by "self-interest," i.e., by their interest in the effective satisfaction of their several wants? Hobbes had presented a radical solution to this problem—the establishment of an absolute sovereign authority—in *Leviathan*, but, as Halévy made clear (Halévy 1901–1904), Hobbes's influence was pushed aside by that of the Lockean wing of the utilitarian tradition, which assumed a "natural identity of interests." The Lockean tradition did not really attempt to solve the problem of order but instead tried to justify the refusal to consider it. Although the Lockean approach facilitated certain valuable developments in economic analysis and in some forms of political analysis, it failed to provide that solution to the problem of order which was needed before a generalized interpretation of modern "economic individualism" could be developed. A notable version of the problem, which greatly influenced Ricardo and indirectly influenced Marx, was advanced by Malthus, but it remained for Durkheim to make a fundamental direct attack on the problem. In terms of substantive sociology, this is the main starting point of his more technical theory.

Before taking this up, however, a few words must be said about the other current of thought converging on the French "middle ground," namely German idealism and the movements stemming from it.

The problems that social science must explain, in Durkheim's view, lie on the subjective side of the Cartesian dichotomy, since the entire main tradition of epistemology, of which Descartes's work was the focal point, virtually limited the external world to the world of objects as understood in terms of the new physical science. (It was, of course, possible—witness biologically based psychology and anthropology—to move into social science from the base of the object world, but this path was relatively unimportant to Durkheim.) Whereas the empiricist utilitarians had used this "subjective" element merely as a reference point for the study of behavior, failing conspicuously to structure it on its own terms, the idealists increasingly focused upon it and tended to treat it as a category of objects. In this respect Kant's philosophy seems to have been transitional, while the Hegelian "objective spirit" (*objektiver Geist*) is the focal idealistic conception relevant here. This conception of *Geist* was primarily cultural, somewhat in the tradition of Platonic Ideas. As such it was *transindividual*, on quite a different level from the discrete wants of utilitarianism.

The Hegelian conception underwent various changes, only two aspects of which require mention here. One was the abandonment of the grandiose Hegelian *Weltgeist* in favor of the more restricted "spirits" of what many late nineteenth-century German scholars called discrete "historical individuals," such as particular cultures or civilizations in particular epochs. This modification was perhaps most consistently expounded by Wilhelm Dilthey. The other was that developed by Marx. As the one who "set Hegel on his head," Marx was ostensibly a materialist rather than an idealist. Nevertheless, his materialism belongs to the idealist tradition in that it treats human culture and motivated action as objects, and it tends to be "historical" in the special sense of handling "history" as a series of ideographic exemptions from treatment in terms of generalized analytical categories.

Durkheim accepted the crucial Cartesian statement of the problem of knowledge in terms of the relation between the knowing subject and the known world of external objects. In his initial orientation he was a Cartesian "rationalist," in the sense that he approached the sociological problem as a problem of knowing "social facts" in terms of their place in the object world. However, as he shifted from the problem of knowledge to that of action, he became *concurrently* concerned with social facts as both the social scientist and the actor in society, as subjects, know them. The problem of the relation between the two references was the core problem of Durkheim's scheme. Thus, although basically Cartesian, this scheme could not be developed without going beyond a Cartesian position in several respects.

Rousseau, as the primary philosopher of "democratic individualism" in his time, influenced Durkheim by his special point of view about the characteristics of social phenomena. While Rousseau shared the frame of reference of natural law and natural rights that was so prominent in the seventeenth and eighteenth centuries (and which, in important respects, came to France from England through Locke), he handled the problem of the social integration of those "born free" into a society without invoking the predominantly coercive sovereign of Hobbes or assuming the natural identity of interests, as did Locke. Rather, he postulated a resolution of interests at the level of integrative action processes in terms of the concept of "will." More than any other, Rousseau's famous concept of the *volonté générale* provided a conception of social solidarity that was

neither economic in the sense of classical economics nor
political in the sense of Hobbes or Austin. It was not a
given "identity" of interests, but one achieved and institutionalized in the course of social process. Comte's concept of
"consensus," which stood more immediately in Durkheim's
background and was explicitly defined as sociological, was
transitional between Rousseau's "general will" and Durkheim's conception of solidarity, which lay at the core of his
sociology.

The problem of order. Durkheim's initial orientation
to the study of society was twofold. The substantive aspect
was developed in the *Division of Labor* and concerned the
problem of order in a type of system we might call economic
individualism. The methodological frame of reference was
developed more fully in the *Rules of Sociological Method*,
published two years later.

The critical starting point of the *Division of Labor* is its
discussion of Herbert Spencer's conception of a system of
contractual relations (*Division of Labor*, book 1, chapter 7).
Durkheim clearly understood that *order* in a concrete
system of contractual relations—in which the market figured
prominently—could not be accounted for in the terms set
forth by Spencer, whom Durkheim treated as a representative utilitarian. Unless controlled by other factors, a
society dominated by the pure pursuit of self-interest would
dissolve into a Hobbesian state of nature, a complete break-
down of order. The other factor or set of factors Durkheim
formulated in two different ways, and on different levels.
Closest to Spencer's analysis was the conception of the
"non-contractual elements of contract," the important idea
that contracts, i.e., the *ad hoc* agreements between parties,
are always subject to generalized norms. These norms are
not open to negotiation between parties: they exist prior
to any such agreements, having evolved over time. In more
comprehensive systems, these rules or norms are part of
the formal law and are enforced by the legal sanctions of
public authority. Their subject matter is the definition of

the interests for which contracts may be entered into (for example, a man may not contract away his basic civil rights), the means by which such interests may legitimately be pursued (in general terms, coercion and fraud are excluded), and the bearing on contracts of interests other than those of the contracting parties (both the public interest and those of third private parties must be protected).

As noted, at one level the institution of contract is a prominent part of the legal system. Durkheim, however, wanted to go behind the establishment of norms by political authority to societal structures that may be said to "underlie" the mobilization of political authority for the enforcement of contracts. He introduced the concept of organic solidarity essentially to designate the capacity of a social system to integrate the diverse interests inherent in qualitative structural differentiation. Durkheim related solidarity, in turn, to a conception of its underlying ground, which he called *conscience collective*—translatable as either collective conscience or collective consciousness. The normative emphasis of the first translation was important to Durkheim himself: the *conscience collective* was a "system of beliefs and sentiments" held in common by the members of a society and defining what their mutual relations ought to be.

Clearly the *conscience collective* is a derivative of Rousseau's "general will" and Comte's "consensus." Equally clearly, it is not purely cognitive in reference. The most important step that Durkheim took beyond his predecessors, however, was to treat solidarity and with it, presumably, the *conscience collective*, not simply as given, but as variable entities. He made a distinction, therefore, between organic solidarity and mechanical solidarity. Organic solidarity is the analytical type characterized by the structural differentiation of the division of labor: modern society represents a case of predominantly organic solidarity. Mechanical solidarity, by contrast, is characterized by uniformity and lack of differentiation. With this distinction, Durkheim from the beginning built both historical—indeed, evolutionary—and comparative dimensions into his sociological analysis (Bellah 1959).

There is an initial difficulty in interpreting the relation between Durkheim's two types of solidarity, on the one hand, and the concept of the *conscience collective*, on the other. Since the *conscience collective* stresses the commonness of the beliefs and sentiments that constitute it, this seems to identify it with mechanical solidarity and suggests that organic solidarity, associated as it is with differentiation in the social structure, must develop at the expense of the *conscience collective*. The broad solution to this difficulty, which becomes clearer in Durkheim's later work, hinges on the functions attributed to values and norms in social systems of different degrees of differentiation. The focus of the *conscience collective* seems to be what we have come to call the values common to the members of any relatively well integrated social system; the sharing of common values is a constant feature of all such systems—at whatever level of differentiation. In the case of mechanical solidarity, these values are not clearly differentiated from the norms through which they are implemented, but in the organic case the norms come to have independent salience. In the relatively less differentiated social systems characterized by mechanical solidarity, common, in the sense of uniform, sentiments tend to be implemented *directly* in collective action, while in the case of organic solidarity the common element lies at a more general level and must be implemented in relation to different functions in the system through norms that are not identical for different sections of the collectivity.

Sociological method. The second main line of development of Durkheim's analysis has to do with the fitting of these broad empirical considerations into what I have called his Cartesian frame of reference. The starting point is the conception of the *actor* as member of a social system and as oriented to the environment in which he acts. This actor, conceived on the model of the philosopher–scientist, observes and interprets the facts of the external world: the distinctive problem is not their status as facts (of the environment), but as *social* facts. Here Durkheim self-consciously and explicitly denied the physical environment its unique "reality." The *milieu social*—for him the relevant environment—is, as part of society, a "reality *sui generis*," to be studied in its own right. The central problem concerns the properties of this category of "reality."

This problem in turn has two principal aspects. From the viewpoint of the scientific observer, this reality is clearly factual, or as we would say, empirical. But what was it from the viewpoint of the actor, in the second sense in which Durkheim was using the Cartesian scheme? A society is a given reality (it has "exteriority") from the point of view of its own members, but it also regulates ("constrains") their action. This it does not only in the sense in which the physical environment sets conditions that action must take into account but also by defining goals and normative standards for action. Durkheim quite early conceived of this constraint as more than a matter of given conditions; he saw it rather as a system of rules enforced by humanly imposed sanctions. In this theoretical development, Durkheim was evidently following up his previous analysis of the law (in the *Division of Labor*) as both an index of the structure of the society (e.g., of the nature and extent of its differentiation) and, when it is considered together with the beliefs and sentiments of the *conscience collective*, as a very important normative component of all societies.

There is, however, a still deeper aspect of the problem. A scientific observer of physical events is not in quite the same sense a "member" of the system he observes as is the social actor, although it is not acceptable to suggest that there is *no* sense in which they are similarly "members." It was necessary, therefore, to relativize the sense in which the system that Durkheim calls society constitutes *only* an environment to the individual actor-members that compose it. This problem, then, came to be intertwined with that of the status of the normative aspects of a society.

The essential conclusion of Durkheim's thinking is that for the sociologist the boundary between "individual" and "society" cannot be that of common sense. If we interpret the former concept as something like the human personality, it must *include* a sector of the social system, most specifically, the normative aspect of that system, the *shared* beliefs and sentiments that constitute the *conscience collective*. By this path Durkheim arrived at the crucially important view that essential elements of culture and social structure are *internalized* as part of the personality of the individual. In this he converged notably with Freud and with the movement in American social psychology from Charles H. Cooley to George Herbert Mead and W. I. Thomas. Durkheim's quite revolutionary conclusion now seems to follow more or less inevitably from his premises, once he tried seriously to fit into the Cartesian frame of reference a distinctive normative level of the social system both as a "reality *sui generis*," for the actor as well as for the observer, and as an environment that is much more than just an environment.

This meant a radical reinterpretation of Durkheim's original criteria of social facts—constraint and exteriority. The concept of social facts was developed, then, through three phases: first, exteriority, or the giveness of empirical existence, as in the case of the physical environment; second, constraint, or the effect of a normative rule to which sanctions are attached; and now, third, what Durkheim called the "moral authority" of internalized values and norms, which "constrain" the individual to conform by arousing guilt in his own conscience if he does not conform. An element of exteriority is involved in moral authority because, although internalized, the normative system must also objectively be part of a system extending beyond the individual. It is not "subjective" in the sense of being purely private to the individual, for it is also a "cultural object" in a sense relevant to the idealistic tradition.

The theoretical development at this highest level of generality—Durkheim's decisively new conception of individuals interacting in a social system—did not fully crystallize until the early years of the present century, when Durkheim gave primary attention to the relations between moral norms and the process of education (1902–1906). Some of its roots in the more empirical emphases of the *Division of Labor* have already been indicated. Certainly the most notable transitional formulation of the concept of social fact is in his study of suicide. Durkheim's sensitivity to the major problems of suicide went back to the *Division of Labor* and its critique of utilitarianism, more specifically the utilitarian claim that an increasing division of labor and the resultant economic progress would be accompanied by increasing "happiness." Durkheim was struck by the fact that the economic progress of newly industrialized societies was everywhere accompanied by a rise in suicide rates. This was clearly an anomaly from the point of view of utilitarian theory and stimulated Durkheim to a major, if not complete, theoretical reconstruction in his classic monograph *Suicide* (1897).

Very advanced for its time as an empirical study, *Suicide* established a most important link between Durkheim's theoretical work and the traditions of empirical research that have since become prominent, especially in the United States. Durkheim's essential method was systematically to mobilize available statistical information on suicide rates and to relate their variations to a whole series of characteristics of the populations involved. In the nature of the case, he was limited to the modern Western world, which alone provided the kind of information he sought. With this limitation, he studied nationality, religion, age, sex, marital status, family size, place of residence, economic status, and variations in economic conditions, as well as the seasons of the year and even the times of day when suicides occurred. He showed great ingenuity and a capacity to take pains— for example, in breaking down the data published for

France by *départements* into *arrondissements*, in order to reveal important variations masked in the larger units. As Bellah points out (Bellah 1959), Durkheim brought together what information he could find from the broadest possible comparative range, even when it could not be stated quantitatively. For instance, he cited voluntary self-immolation on the part of Buddhist zealots as an example of what he called "altruistic" suicide.

Durkheim found the conventional classification of the "causes" of suicide, in terms of which the data were generally reported, quite unhelpful for his purposes. He introduced a highly original scheme of his own, built about the problem of the individual's relations to the normative structuring of the social system in which he is involved. This scheme embodies two pairs of polar extremes, at which suicide rates are relatively high, and median continua between the poles, in which suicide rates are relatively low. The first pair of poles has *altruisme* and *égoïsme* at the extremes, the second *anomie* and *fatalisme*.

That Durkheim was no mere extoller of the virtues of solidarity (as is sometimes alleged) is shown by his conception of the first polar pair in general and of the concept of "altruistic" suicide in particular. In this type the claims of the collectivity are so strong that there is a repeated tendency to subordinate personal interests to them to the extent of sacrificing life, even when there does not appear to be a practical emergency that requires such sacrifice. Durkheim found military officers most prone to this in modern societies, but adduced numerous other examples from other societies. The antithesis of this type is "egoistic" suicide, which, for example, results in a higher rate of suicide among Protestants than among Catholics. This Durkheim explained by the social pressure inherent in Protestant norms toward a higher order of individual religious responsibility. It is a remarkable interpretation, both in itself and because it converges with the theme developed a few years later by Max Weber concerning the importance of the Protestant ethic in modern society. There is also, interestingly, an echo of Rousseau, in that Durkheim seemed to be citing an instance of the famous paradoxical formula about a man being "forced to be free," adding that this enforced freedom may become too hard to bear.

The second pair of polar concepts that Durkheim advanced in this connection was that of *anomie* and *fatalisme* (the latter concept not being developed). Anomie has become one of the small number of truly central concepts of contemporary social science. It is best interpreted in terms of Durkheim's Cartesian reference. The observer as actor is naturally concerned with the definiteness of the "reality" with which he is confronted. In a purely cognitive context, this is a matter of the adequacy of his information and analysis. Insofar, however, as the "reality" is man-made and, in one aspect, is normative *for* the actor, the problem of definiteness becomes that of "definition of the situation" in the sense established by W. I. Thomas and by reference-group theory more generally [*see* REFERENCE GROUPS].

The focus, then, is on what is *expected* of the actor and on the problem of the definiteness of expectations. In the case of the physical conditions of, for example, technological procedures, expectations can reasonably be defined in terms of the goals of the actors: they do not pertain to the external processes and technically defined probabilities concerning the environment itself, since it does not "act." In a system of social interaction, on the other hand, "success" cannot simply be a function of "control" over the environment, but necessarily involves also the "sense" it makes to exert effort and, generally, to expend resources, unless the outcome to which the actor is committed is clearly desirable. The sense to ego of his goal-striving is thus a function both of alter's action and of ego's expectation concerning it. The meaning of success cannot be established without understanding the interplay between the motivation of the actor and the normative claims impinging upon him from his social environment. At the same time, the social environment of any *given* actor of reference is composed of *other* actors whose action must be analyzed in the same terms as the first. In this interactive framework anomie may be considered that state of a social system which makes a particular class of members consider exertion for success meaningless, not because they lack capacity or opportunity to achieve what is wanted, but because they lack a clear definition of what is desirable. It is a "pathology" not of the instrumental system but of the collective normative system.

Spelling out this concept leads to many refinements. In more contemporary terms, what is ill-defined may be ultimate beliefs, values, norms, or goals. Anomic uncertainty may affect either very generalized orientations or relatively specific goals; or the difficulties may arise from conflicting expectations, as in the classic instance of "cross-pressures."

The two concepts of *égoïsme* and *anomie* epitomize Durkheim's concern over the state of modern society. Because of the current preoccupation with problems of "meaning" in contemporary life, it is not surprising that *anomie* has attracted far more attention than *égoïsme*. It is my own view that the balance is in need of being redressed. *Égoïsme*, in Durkheim's special sense, is a designation for one aspect of a prominent feature of modern social structure that can be called, more generally, "institutionalized individualism." Another context in which Durkheim emphasized *égoïsme* was his discussion of the "cult of individual personality" (Neyer 1960). At least some aspects of the subject of "alienation" (discussed so often and with so much confusion) may also be interpreted in terms of *égoïsme* and *altruisme*. Thus, alienation appears to be the pathological extreme (anomic in certain aspects, cf. Tiryakian 1962) of institutionalized individualism at which "conformism" becomes associated with the altruistic tendencies, in Durkheim's sense. The alienated person, then, is under such pressure to establish his independence from pressures to conform that he becomes unable to accept the essential normative conditions of a stable *system* of organized individual freedom.

Theory of culture. In the last major phase of his intellectual career, Durkheim dealt mainly with another set of themes that grew out of, but were distinct from, those outlined so far. These concerned religion, symbolic systems, and his somewhat new conception, "collective representations." In short, he emphasized the theory of culture in relation to that of the social system. As early as the Preface to Volume 2 of *L'année sociologique* (1899), Durkheim acknowledged the strong emphasis on religion in that publication and outlined his conception of religion as the primordial "matrix," out of which the principal elements of culture emerged by the process of differentiation. His concern with primitive religion, as well as with an articulated evolutionary perspective, was already clear in this statement. It is important for these later developments in Durkheim's thought that the relatively new science of anthropology had arisen as a kind of mediator between utilitarianism and Darwinian biology. Anthropology became the "study of man" as part of the organic world, concerned especially with primitive societies, particularly with their magic and religion.

We have noted that Durkheim's conception of society as a "reality *sui generis*" steadily changed; he placed an increasing emphasis on the normative components. While the legal norms constituted his initial prototype, he gradually focused upon more general aspects, moving toward the conception of what we would now call institutionalized values. He particularly stressed the attitude of moral respect as a component of internalized norms.

What is perhaps Durkheim's most important single step in extending this perspective was stated as one of the primary orienting perspectives of the *Elementary Forms*. This was a double proposition: first, that the attitudinal distinction between treating things as sacred and as profane is basically the same as that between moral obligations and expediency or utility; and second, that the quality of sacredness does not reside in the intrinsic properties of the object treated as sacred, but in its properties as a *symbol*. From this it was a short step to relate sacred physical and social objects to the whole world of "cultural" objects, which, although very close to Durkheim's early category of beliefs and sentiments, he increasingly formulated as "representations." We may certainly interpret them as symbolic systems, leaving open the question of the meaning references of various categories of symbols.

Durkheim was greatly impressed by the closeness of integration between the religious system of representations and the structure of the society itself, the attitude of moral respect being, as noted, the main connecting link. This integration seems particularly close in the case of primitive religion but it also exists in others. It justifies Durkheim's emphasis on collective representations. Indeed, we can say that any symbolic system that can justifiably be called "cultural" must have a collective aspect; symbolization that is autistic—in the sense of being wholly private to one individual (the limiting case)—is no longer cultural, if indeed it can be truly symbolic. Language is perhaps the prototype here.

It seems to have been Durkheim's view, a strongly defensible one, that the more primitive the society and the culture, the less differentiated they are from each other. He extensively analyzed the case of the Australian aborigines on the strength of this theory: the phenomena of the integration of culture and society could be seen there in their "elementary forms." But his interest in these elementary forms does not mean that Durkheim did not have a broad understanding of the possibility and importance of differentiating conceptually between cultural and social systems, even though, as Bellah points out (Bellah 1959), he somewhat obscured this vital point by using the term "social" for both. Unfortunately, he never worked out a thorough analysis of the place of religion in a highly differentiated society—a task that might well have led him to clarify his conception of the relations between "representations" and social structure.

The problem of integration also arises internally to the system of collective representations, to culture itself. Durkheim presented the broad perspective on this problem several years before *Elementary Forms* in the monograph on primitive classification written in collaboration with Mauss (1903), although he developed it further in his book. His main point is that in primitive systems all culture is at the same time both religious and social, in a sense not true of more advanced systems. A particularly telling example is the categorization of physical space in terms directly corresponding to the arrangement of kinship groups in the camp.

This conception of twofold integration, between a cultural and a social system and among the different elements of a cultural system, is particularly significant for the broad problem area we now generally call the sociology of knowledge. Undoubtedly Durkheim was at least as important a founder of this discipline as was Karl Mannheim, and in many respects his views were the clearer and better analyzed.

Durkheim's combined interest in cultural problems, religion, and evolutionary origins had a series of implications for the development of social science theory. Both the utilitarian tradition and that stemming from the French Enlightenment had tended not only to disparage traditional religion but even to deny its substantive importance. Evolutionary perspectives, however, focused attention on religion, partly because of the sheer empirical prominence of religion and magic in nonliterate societies, which were becoming increasingly well-known. The early Tylor–Spencer phase of social science tended strongly to consider these phenomena characteristic of the early stages of sociocultural evolution and destined to disappear with advancement— a position shared by Marx. Durkheim's position established a quite new order of functional significance for religion in society. Durkheim made it clear that even at the later stages of sociocultural development, every society would require the "functional equivalent" of a religious system (whether or not it is called "religion" is primarily a semantic issue).

Beyond this, Durkheim established the groundwork for an exceedingly valuable conception of the morphology of social development—the conception of processes of structural differentiation and of attendant new, more general levels of integration. The conception of religion as the original matrix of both society and culture suggests further that society and culture themselves tend to become more completely differentiated from each other and that "secular" elements develop from this matrix on both the social and cultural levels. An important semantic point is that just because a relatively undifferentiated complex is called "religion" for an earlier stage of development and only one of its two or more differentiated derivatives retains that name for a later stage, it is not legitimate to assert that "religion has declined." Thus, Durkheim viewed the secularization of education as an imperative of the stage of social differentiation that France had reached in his time, but he denied that this meant that the function of religion in French society had therefore been downgraded.

Durkheim's combination of a comparative and evolutionary perspective with a special concern for cultural–symbolic systems should have been connected with a theoretical analysis of the processes of social and cultural change. Durkheim did not, to be sure, give this as much explicit attention as he did problems of social morphology, but the contributions he did make to an understanding of the process of change seem not to have been understood as fully as his more "static" analysis. In any case, it is clear that Durkheim provided the groundwork for a major theory of developmental change in societies and that he made important direct contributions to it himself.

His later work, in particular, tended to stress the importance of cultural creativity as a factor in change: one of the clearest statements is in his late essay "Value Judgments and Judgments of Reality" (1911), which stresses the incidence and salience of "effervescence" in periods of crisis in the development of the sociocultural system. At the same time, Durkheim was quite clearly a "multifactor" theorist of social change.

Conclusion. Durkheim contributed substantially—and very eminently for the time in which he worked—to relatively specific empirical problems in sociology. To this day, analyses of the nature of contractual systems, of suicide rates, and of primitive religions cannot ignore his contributions. Equally, he was a highly effective entrepreneur of sociology—as teacher, as editor of a distinguished periodical, and as leader of a highly talented and creative group of research scholars.

These are not, however, the achievements that place him in the top rank among the founders of a scientific discipline. This higher eminence stems from the fact that Durkheim used the framework of solidly established intellectual traditions—those of English utilitarianism, in certain respects of German idealism, and of his own French background—to formulate a theoretical framework that was both solidly grounded in those traditions and yet highly original. As grounded in tradition, it was capable of taking full account of established knowledge; but it also went far beyond this. It was precise and clear in its logical structures and imaginative in opening up new ways of considering social phenomena, defining problems, and developing patterns of interpretation. In his special conception of the nature of "social reality," which emphasized the involvement of *normative components* in both social reality and, through internalization, the personality of the individual, Durkheim was following, along with a few others, the major line of the theoretical development of social science. But he went even beyond this to link the social and personality systems thus conceived with a highly sophisticated analysis of cultural symbolic systems and to set the whole action structure in a comprehensive evolutionary framework. The resulting enrichment of the theoretical resources of the field of social science, of its insight into significant problems and its capacity to deal determinately with them, is incalculable. Only a very select few among the figures in intellectual history have contributed so crucially—at such a significant juncture—to the development of scientific culture.

* * *

WORKS BY DURKHEIM

1888 "Cours de science sociale: Leçon d'ouverture." *Revue Internationale de L'enseignement*, XV, 23–48.

1888 "Introduction à la sociologie de la famille." *Annales de la faculté des lettres de Bordeaux*, pp. 257–281.

1889 "Tönnies, F., *Gemeinschaft und Gesellschaft.*" *Revue Philosophique*, XXVII, 416–422.

1890 "Les Principes de 1789 et la sociologie." *Revue Internationale de L'enseignement*, XIX, 450–456.

1890 "La Famille conjugale: Conclusion du cours sur la famille." *Revue Philosophique*, XCI (1921), 1–14.

(1893) 1947 *The Division of Labor in Society*. Glencoe, Ill.: Free Press. → First published as *De la division du travail social*. → A paperback edition was published in 1964 by The Free Press.

(1895) 1958 *The Rules of Sociological Method*. 8th ed. Edited by George E. G. Catlin. Glencoe, Ill.: Free Press. → First published in French.

(1896) 1958 *Socialism and Saint-Simon*. Translated by Charlotte Sattler, edited and with an introduction by Alvin W. Gouldner. Yellow Springs, Ohio: Antioch Press. → First published in 1928 as *Le Socialisme: Sa définition, ses débuts, la doctrine Saint-Simonienne*.

(1897) 1951 *Suicide: A Study in Sociology*. Glencoe, Ill.: Free Press. → First published in French. → A paperback edition was published in 1966 by The Free Press.

1897 "La Prohibition de l'inceste et ses origines." *L'année Sociologique*, I, 1–70.

(1898–1911) 1953 *Sociology and Philosophy*. Glencoe, Ill.: Free Press. → Written between 1898–1911. First published in French in 1924.

1898 "L'Individualisme et les intellectuels." *Revue Bleue*, Series 4, X, 7–13.

1898 "De la définition des phénomènes religieux." *L'année Sociologique*, II, 1–28.

(1899) 1960 Prefaces to *L'année Sociologique*: Preface to Volume 2. Pages 347–353 in Kurt H. Wolff (editor), *Emile Durkheim, 1858–1917: A Collection of Essays With Translations and a Bibliography*. Columbus: Ohio State Univ. Press.

(1900) 1957 *Professional Ethics and Civic Morals*. Translated by Cornelia Brookfield. London: Routledge and Kegan Paul. → First published in French in 1950 as *Leçons de sociologie: Physique des moeurs et du droit*.

1900 "Deux lois de l'évolution pénale." *L'année Sociologique*, IV, 65–95.

(1901) 1960 "Rousseau's Social Contract," in *Montesquieu and Rousseau: Forerunners of Sociology*. Translated by Ralph Manheim. Ann Arbor: University of Michigan Press. → First published in French in 1918 as "Le Contrat social de Rousseau."

(1902) 1956 "Pedagogy and sociology," in *Education and Sociology*. Translated, with an introduction, by Sherwood D. Fox. Glencoe, Ill.: Free Press. → First published in French as "Pédagogie et sociologie."

(1902–1906) 1961 *Moral Education: A Study in the Theory and Application of the Sociology of Education*. New York: Free Press. → Lectures first published in French. → A paperback edition was published by The Free Press in 1973.

(1903) 1963 DURKHEIM, EMILE; and MAUSS, MARCEL. *Primitive Classification*. Translated and edited by Rodney Needham. Univ. of Chicago Press. → First published as "De quelques formes primitives de classification" in *L'année Sociologique*.

(1905) 1938 *L'Evolution pédagogique en France*, 2 vols. Paris: Félix Alcan.

(1906) 1953 The Determination of Moral Facts. Pages 35–62 in Emile Durkheim, *Sociology and Philosophy*. Glencoe, Ill.: Free Press. → First published in French.

1909 "Sociologie religieuse et théorie de la connaissance." *Revue de Métaphysique et de Morale*, XVII, 733–758.

1900 Discussion of "L'Efficacité des doctrines morales." Séance du 20 mai, 1909. *Bulletin de la société française de philosophie*, IX, 193–231, *passim*.

1900 Discussion of "La Notion d'égalité sociale." Séance du 30 décembre, 1909. *Bulletin de la société française de philosophie*, X, 58–80, *passim*.

(1911) 1953 Value Judgments and Judgments of Reality. Pages 80–97 in Emile Durkheim, *Sociology and Philosophy*. Glencoe, Ill.: Free Press. → First published in French.

(1912) 1954 *The Elementary Forms of the Religious Life*. London: Allen & Unwin; New York: Macmillan. → First published as *Les formes élémentaires de la vie religieuse, le système totémique en Australie*. A paperback edition was published in 1954 by The Free Press.

(1914) 1955 *Pragmatisme et sociologie*. Paris: J. Vrin.

(1914) 1960 "The Dualism of Human Nature and Its Social Conditions." Translated by Charles Blend. In *Emile Durkheim, 1858–1917*. Edited by Kurt H. Wolff. Columbus, Ohio: Ohio State University Press. → First published in French as "Le Dualisme de la nature humaine et ses conditions sociales."

1915 "La Sociologie." *La Science française*, Vol. I. Paris: Librairie Larousse.

(1917) 1920 "Introduction à la morale." *Revue Philosophique*, LXXXIX, 79-97.

(1917) 1919 "La 'Pédagogie' de Rousseau." *Revue de Métaphysique et de Morale*, XXVI, 153–180.

WORKS ABOUT DURKHEIM

ALPERT, HARRY (1939) 1961 *Emile Durkheim and His Sociology*. New York: Russell.

ARON, RAYMOND 1965 *Main Currents in Sociological Thought*. 2 vols. New York: Basic Books.

BECKER, HOWARD; and BARNES, HARRY E. (1938) 1961 *Social Thought From Lore to Science*. 3d ed., rev. & enl. New York: Dover. See especially Volume 2, Chapter 12.

BELLAH, ROBERT N. 1959 Durkheim and History. *American Sociological Review* 24:447–461.

BELLAH, ROBERT N. 1970 *Beyond Belief*. New York: Harper and Row.

BELLAH, ROBERT N. 1973 *Emile Durkheim on Morality and Society.* Heritage of Sociology Series. Chicago, Ill.: University of Chicago Press.

BERGER, PETER L.; and LUCKMANN, THOMAS 1967 *The Social Construction of Reality.* Garden City, N.Y.: Doubleday and Company, Inc.

BERGSON, HENRI 1935 *The Two Sources of Morality.* Translated by R. Ashley Audra and Cloudesley Brereton. Garden City, N.Y.: Doubleday and Company, Inc.

BIERSTEDT, ROBERT 1966 *Emile Durkheim.* London: Weidenfeld and Nicolson.

BLACK, MAX, ed. 1961 *The Social Theories of Talcott Parsons.* Englewood Cliffs, N.J.: Prentice-Hall.

BOUGLÉ, CÉLESTIN 1938 *Bilan de la sociologie française contemporaine.* Paris: Félix Alcan.

CLARK, TERRY N. 1973 *Prophets and Patrons: The French University and the Emergence of the Social Sciences.* Cambridge, Mass.: Harvard Univ. Press.

COSER, LEWIS 1956 *The Functions of Social Conflict.* New York: Free Press. → A paperback edition was published in 1964 by The Free Press.

COULANGES, FUSTEL de 1955 *The Ancient City.* Garden City, N.Y.: Doubleday and Company, Inc.

DAVY, GEORGES 1960 Emile Durkheim. *Revue française de sociologie* 1:3–24.

DAVY, GEORGES 1919 and 1920 Emile Durkheim. *Revue de Métaphysique et de Morale* XXVI:181–198 and XXVII:71–112

DAVY, GEORGES 1911 "La sociologie de M. Durkheim." *Revue Philosophique* LXXXII:47–71, 160–185.

DENNES, WILLIAM RAY 1924 *The Methods and Presuppositions of Group Psychology.* University of California Publications in Philosophy, No. 6. Berkeley and Los Angeles: University of California Press.

EISENSTADT, S. N., ed. 1968 *The Protestant Ethic and Modernization.* New York: Basic Books, Inc.

EVANS-PRITCHARD, E. E. 1962 *Social Anthropology and Other Essays.* Glencoe, Ill.: Free Press. → A paperback edition was published in 1964 by The Free Press.

GEHLKE, CHARLES E. 1915 *Emile Durkheim's Contributions to Sociological Theory.* New York: Columbia Univ. Press.

GIDDENS, ANTHONY 1971 *Capitalism and Modern Social Theory: An Analysis of the Writings of Marx, Durkheim, and Max Weber.* Cambridge, England: Cambridge University Press.

GIDDENS, ANTHONY, ed. 1972 *Emile Durkheim: Selected Writings.* Translated by A. Giddens. London: Cambridge University Press.

GOLDENWEISER, ALEXANDER A. 1958 Religion and Society: A Critique of Durkheim's Theory of the Origin and Nature of Religion. In *Reader in Comparative Religion,* 2d ed. Edited by William A. Lessa and Evon Z. Vogt. New York: Harper and Row.

GURVITCH, GEORGES 1937 La science des faits moraux et la morale théoretique chez E. Durkheim. *Archives de philosophie du droit et de sociologie juridique* [1937], no. 1/2:18–44.

GURVITCH, GEORGES (1950) 1957–1963 *La vocation actuelle de la sociologie.* 2d ed., 2 vols. Paris: Presses Universitaires de France. → Volume 1: *Vers la sociologie différentielle.* Volume 2: *Antécédents et perspectives.*

HALBWACHS, MAURICE 1918 La doctrine d'Emile Durkheim. *Revue philosophique de la France et de l'étranger* 85:353–411.

HALÉVY, ELIE (1901–1904) 1952 *The Growth of Philosophic Radicalism.* New ed. London: Faber. → First published in French.

HUGHES, HENRY STUART 1958 *Consciousness and Society: The Reorientation of European Social Thought, 1890–1930.* New York: Knopf.

LA CAPRA, DOMINICK 1972 *Emile Durkheim.* Ithaca, N.Y.: Cornell Univ. Press.

LÉVI-STRAUSS, CLAUDE 1945 French Sociology. Pages 503–537 in Georges Gurvitch and Wilbert E. Moore (editors), *Twentieth Century Sociology.* New York: Philosophical Library.

LUKES, STEVEN 1972 *Emile Durkheim, His Life and Work: A Historical and Critical Study.* New York: Harper and Row.

MALINOWSKI, BRONISLAW (1916–1941) 1948 *Magic, Science and Religion, and Other Essays.* Glencoe, Ill.: Free Press. → A paperback edition was published in 1954 by Doubleday.

MAUSS, MARCEL 1923 In Memoriam: l'oeuvre inédite de Durkheim et de ses collaborateurs. *Année sociologique,* New Series, 1:7–29.

MAUSS, MARCEL 1950 *Sociologie et anthropologie.* Paris: Presses Universitaires de France.

MERTON, ROBERT K. 1934 Durkheim's *Division of Labor in Society. American Journal of Sociology* 40:319–328.

MERTON, ROBERT K. (1938) 1957 Social Structure and Anomie. Pages 131–160 in Robert K. Merton, *Social Theory and Social Structure.* Rev. & enl. ed. Glencoe, Ill.: Free Press.

NAEGELE, K. D. 1958 Attachment and Alienation: Complementary Aspects of the Work of Durkheim and Simmel. *American Journal of Sociology* LXIII: 580–589.

NEYER, JOSEPH 1960 Individualism and Socialism in Durkheim. Pages 32–76 in Kurt H. Wolff (editor), *Emile Durkheim, 1858–1917: A Collection of Essays With Translations and a Bibliography.* Columbus: Ohio State Univ. Press.

NISBET, ROBERT A. 1965 *Emile Durkheim.* Englewood Cliffs, N.J.: Prentice-Hall, Inc.

NISBET, ROBERT A. 1974 *The Sociology of Emile Durkheim.* New York: Oxford University Press.

PARSONS, TALCOTT 1937 *The Structure of Social Action.* New York: McGraw-Hill.

PARSONS, TALCOTT 1965 Unity and Diversity in the Modern Intellectual Disciplines: The Role of the Social Sciences. *Daedalus* 94: 39–65.

PARSONS, TALCOTT 1973 Durkheim on Religion Revisited: Another Look at *The Elementary Forms of the Religious Life.* Pages 156–180 in Charles Y. Glock and Phillip E. Hammond (editors), *Essays in the Scientific Study of Religion.* New York: Harper and Row.

PARSONS, TALCOTT; SHILS, EDWARD; NAEGELE, K. D.; and PITTS, JESSE R. 1961 *Theories of Society,* Vols. I and II. Glencoe, Ill.: Free Press.

PEYRE, HENRI 1960 Durkheim: The Man, His Time, and His Intellectual Background. Pages 3–31 in Kurt H. Wolff (editor), *Emile Durkheim, 1858–1917: A Collection of Essays With Translations and a Bibliography.* Columbus: Ohio State Univ. Press.

POGGI, G. 1972 *Images of Society: Essays on the Sociological Theories of Tocqueville, Marx, and Durkheim.* Stanford, Calif.: Stanford University Press.

SIMPSON, GEORGE 1933 Emile Durkheim's Social Realism. *Sociology and Social Research* 18: 2–11.

SOROKIN, PITIRIM A. 1928 *Contemporary Sociological Theories.* New York: Harper. → A paperback edition was published in 1964 as *Contemporary Sociological Theories Through the First Quarter of the Twentieth Century.*

TIRYAKIAN, EDWARD A. 1962 *Sociologism and Existentialism: Two Perspectives on the Individual and Society.* Englewood Cliffs, N.J.: Prentice-Hall.

WALLWORK, ERNEST E. 1972 *Durkheim: Morality and Milieu.* Cambridge, Mass.: Harvard University Press.

WOLFF, KURT H. (editor) 1960 *Emile Durkheim, 1858–1917: A Collection of Essays With Translations and a Bibliography.* Columbus: Ohio State Univ. Press. → A paperback edition was published in 1964 by Harper as *Essays on Sociology and Philosophy, With Appraisals of Durkheim's Life and Thought.*

I

INDIVIDUAL AND COLLECTIVE REPRESENTATIONS[1]

IF analogy is not a method of demonstration in the true sense of the word, it is nevertheless a method of illustration and of secondary verification which may be of some use. It is always interesting to see whether a law established for one order of facts may not, *mutatis mutandis*, be found to apply elsewhere. This comparison may also serve to confirm it and give a greater understanding of its implications. In fact, analogy is a legitimate form of comparison, and comparison is the only practical means we have for the understanding of things. The fault of the biological sociologists was not that they used it but that they used it wrongly. Instead of trying to control their studies of society by their knowledge of biology, they tried to infer the laws of the first from the laws of the second. Such inferences are worthless. If the laws governing natural life are found also in society, they are found in different forms and with specific characteristics which do not permit of conjecture by analogy and can only be understood by direct observation. However, if one had already by the use of sociological methods begun to determine certain qualities of social organization, it would be perfectly legitimate to inquire afterwards whether these qualities did not show some partial similarities with the animal organism as established by the biologist. It might be assumed that all organisms must have certain characteristics in common which are worth while studying.

It is, however, much more natural to look for analogies

[1] First published in *Revue de Métaphysique et de Morale*, vol. vi, May, 1898.

which may exist between the laws of sociology and those of
psychology, because these two cover neighbouring fields.
Like the individual, the collective life is composed of
representations, and it may therefore be presumed that
collective and individual representations are in some ways
comparable. We shall in fact try to show that both maintain
the same relations with their respective substrata. Far from
justifying the belief that reduces sociology to nothing more
than a corollary of individual psychology, this similarity
will on the contrary set in relief the relative independence
of the two worlds and the two sciences.

I

The psychological conceptions of Huxley and Maudsley,
which reduce the mind to nothing more than an epiphenomenon of physical life, have no longer many defenders; even the most authoritative representatives of the
psycho-physiological school have formally rejected them
and endeavoured to show that such conceptions are not
implicit in their principles. The fact of the matter is that
the cardinal idea of this system is purely verbal. Certain
phenomena have a limited efficacy—that is to say, they only
affect surrounding phenomena slightly; but the idea of an
added phenomenon which has no purpose, which does
nothing, lacks all positive content. Even the metaphors
which the theoreticians of this school employ most frequently to express their meaning turn against them. They
say that the mind is a simple reflection of the underlying
cerebral processes. It is a light which accompanies, but
does not constitute, those processes. But a light is not a
'nothing', it is a reality which testifies to its presence by its
peculiar effects. Objects are not the same and do not act
in the same way according to whether they are in the light
or not; light can even alter their characteristics. In the
same way the act of understanding, however imperfectly,
the organic process which one wishes to make the essence

of psychic facts constitutes a new reality which is not without importance, and which manifests itself by noticeable signs. The more this faculty for understanding what happens within ourselves is developed, the more the subject's movements lose that automatism which is the characteristic of physical life. The agent endowed with reason does not behave like a thing of which the activity can be reduced to a system of reflexes. He hesitates, feels his way, deliberates, and by that distinguishing mark he is recognized. External stimulation, instead of resulting immediately in movements, is halted in its progress and is subjected to a *sui generis* elaboration; a more or less long period of time elapses before the expression in movement appears. This relative indetermination does not occur where there is no thinking mind, and with thought it increases. It would appear, then, that the reason (*la conscience*) is not as inert as has been supposed. Indeed, how could it be otherwise? All that is has its specific way of being and has its peculiar properties. But every property expresses itself by manifestations which could not occur had that property been other than it is, for it is by this behaviour that the property is defined. Thus whatever name one may give to the reason, it has certain qualities without which it would not be recognizable. Consequently from the moment that it exists things cannot occur as though it did not.

The same objection can be put in the following form. It is a commonplace of both science and philosophy that everything is subject to becoming. But change produces effects. Even the most passive participates in the stimulus which it receives, if only by resisting. Its life and direction depend in part upon its weight, its molecular constitution, etc. If, then, all change implies a certain causal ability in what is changing, and if the mind once produced is incapable of producing anything, we are forced to the conclusion that from the moment it exists it ceases to be subject to change. It would stay as it is; the series of transformations of which it is a part would stop with it, and beyond it there would be nothing more. It would be in a sense the final stage of reality, *finis ultimus naturae*. It is not necessary to point out that such a notion is untenable, for it contradicts all the principles of science. The way in which representations are destroyed would become equally unintelligible from this point of view, for any compound which dissolves is always, to a certain extent, a factor in its own dissolution.

It seems to us useless to discuss any further a system which, taken literally, is contradictory in its terms. Since observation has revealed the existence of an order of phenomena called representations, distinguishable by certain characteristics from all other natural phenomena, it is scarcely methodical to treat them as though they did not exist. Undoubtedly they are caused, but they are in their turn causes. Life itself is nothing but a combination of mineral particles; nobody, however, tries to make it an epiphenomenon of inorganic matter. Once this proposition has been accepted we must also accept the logical consequences. But it is a fundamental proposition which seems to have escaped several psychologists and we shall endeavour to throw a little light upon it.

The reduction of the memory to an organic fact has become almost classical. The representation, it is maintained, has no power of retaining itself as such. When a sensation, image, or idea is no longer presented to us it ceases to exist, without leaving the slightest trace. The organic impression which preceded the representation does not, however, disappear completely. What remains is a modification of the nerve elements involved which will predispose them to vibrate again as they vibrated on the first occasion. Subjected to any further stimulus this same vibration will be reproduced; there results in the mind the psychic state which appeared before, in the same conditions, at the time of the first experience. The memory results from and consists in this process. That this renewed state appears to us as a revivification of the first is then only an illusion. Indeed, if the theory is exact it is an entirely new phenomenon. It is not the old sensation reawakened after lying dormant for some time; it must be an entirely new sensation in so far as nothing remains of the original one. If it did not by a recognized process locate itself in the past, we would really believe that we had never before experienced it. The only thing which is the *same* in the two experiences is the state of the nerves, the necessary condition of the second representation as of the first. This theory is not maintained only by the psycho-physiological school. It is also explicitly admitted by many psychologists who believe in the reality of the mind and wish to see in mental life the highest form of reality. Thus Léon Dumont says: 'When we no longer entertain an idea it no longer exists, even in a latent condition. Only one of its conditions remains and serves to explain how, with other conditions, the same thought may be renewed.' A particular act of memory results 'from the combination of two elements: (i) a condition in the organism complemented by (ii) a force coming from without'.[1] Rabier, writing in almost the same terms, says: 'The action of memory is a new stimulus to the habituated conditions, having the effect of restoring a state of the nerve centres (an impression) similar to, although usually weaker than, that which produced the original representation.'[2] William James is more formal still. 'The phenomenon of "retention"', he says, 'is not a fact of the mental order at all. It is a purely physical phenomenon, a morphological feature, the presence of these "paths" namely, in the finest recesses of the brain's tissue.'[3]

The representation follows the restimulation of the affected area just as it followed the original stimulus, but in the interval it has completely ceased to exist. Nobody

[1] 'De l'habitude', in *Revue Philosophique*, I, pp. 350-1.
[2] *Leçons de Philosophie*, I, p. 164.
[3] *Principles of Psychology*, I, p. 655.

insists more than James upon the duality of these states and upon their heterogeneity. There is nothing common to them except the traces left in the cerebral tissues by the first excitation, which make the second more smooth and rapid.[1] The consequence, moreover, follows logically from the principles of this explanation.

But how is it that James has failed to see that thus he is in agreement with Maudsley, whose theory he has earlier rejected with contempt?[2] If at each moment of time the psychic life consists exclusively in the actual condition present in the mind, one is justified in saying that the mental life is reduced to nothing. It is agreed that the field of the mind's activity is, as Wundt says, very limited; its elements can be enumerated. If, then, they are the only psychic factors in our conduct, we are forced to conclude that our conduct is entirely dependent upon physical causes. Our direction is guided not by the few ideas that hold our attention, but by the residues of our past: the habits which we have contracted, the prejudices, the tendencies which motivate us and for which we cannot completely account to ourselves—in a word, all that constitutes our moral character. If, then, nothing of all this is mental, if the past cannot exist within us except in material form, it is indeed the organism that leads the man. For however much of the past the mind can conceive at any given moment it is nothing in the light of that which cannot be conceived and, further, the number of entirely new impressions is infinitesimal. Moreover, pure sensation, in so far as it exists, is of all intellectual phenomena the one to which the term epiphenomenon could the most properly be applied. It is clear that it depends very closely on the disposition of the organs, as long as another mental phenomenon does not intervene and modify it, in which case it ceases to be pure sensation.

[1] Ibid., p. 656.
[2] Ibid., pp. 145, 188. [He rejects Spencer on p. 145, Comte on p. 188, and deals rather roughly with Maudsley on p. 656.—D. F. P.]

Let us, however, go further and consider what in fact happens in the mind. Could it be said at least that the mental states have a specific nature, that they are subject to special laws, and that if their influence is slight, due to their numerical inferiority, they are, for all that, none the less original? The actual effect upon the action of the vital forces would not amount to much, but it would be something. But how could it be possible? The very life of these features consists in the *sui generis* manner in which they are grouped. It would be necessary for them to be attracted and to associate together according to the affinities of their intrinsic natures rather than the characteristics and organization of the nervous system. If, then, the memory is organic, these associations must be reflections of equally organic connexions. For if a representation cannot be evoked except through the antecedent physical condition, and this latter cannot be revived except by a physical cause, ideas cannot be linked unless the corresponding points in the cerebral mass are materially linked. This, in fact, is expressly maintained by the partisans of the theory. In deducing this corollary from their principle we have done no violence to their thought, since we attribute to them nothing that they do not admit, as indeed they are logically bound to do. As James himself says,[1] 'the psychological law of association [of objects thought of through their previous contiguity in thought or experience[2]] would thus be an effect within the mind of the physical fact that nerve currents propagate themselves most easily through those tracts of conduction which have already been most in use'. And M. Rabier: 'In an association of ideas the suggestive feature *a* has its corresponding condition, the neural impression A; the suggested feature *b* has another neural impression, B. This being accepted, to explain how these two modifications, and consequently these two states of mind, follow each other is only a short step, which is to conclude that *the neural agitation has spread from A to B*; and because the

[1] Op. cit., I, p. 563.   [2] From the original not quoted by Durkheim.

movement has followed this trajectory once it will find the same path easier in the future.'[1]

But if the mental association is only an 'echo' of the physical association, what use is it? Why does not the nervous movement immediately determine the muscular movement without the intervention of this phantom-like mind? Will our earlier arguments be raised to the effect that this 'echo' has its reality and that a molecular vibration in conjunction with a conscious mind is not the same as one without the mind, that, in fact, a new entity is in existence? The defenders of the epiphenomenalist theory use the same argument. They also know very well that an unconscious cerebral process differs from what they call a conscious cerebral process. The problem is, however, whether this difference is in the nature of the process itself —in, for example, the intensity of the neural agitation—or whether it is due to the addition of the mind. If this addition is not redundant, the new factor which has now been added, the mind, must have some activity peculiar to itself and can, in fact, produce effects which cannot occur in its absence. But if, as is supposed, the laws that govern it are the same as those that govern neural matter, they can only be a useless repetition of the latter. We cannot even suppose that this combination, while only reproducing certain cerebral processes, nevertheless gives birth to a new state with a relative autonomy which is more than a pure succedaneum of some organic phenomenon. For according to the hypothesis such a state cannot last unless it is essentially based in a polarization of the cerebral cells. What is a state of mind that has no persistence?

Generally speaking, if a representation can exist only when it is supported by certain conditions of intensity and quality in the neural elements and disappears if this is not sustained, it can have no reality of its own which does not derive directly from its substratum. As Maudsley and his school have maintained, it is a shadow which no longer

[1] Op. cit., I, 195.

exists when the object it reproduces is no longer there. From which one concludes that there is no real mental life and consequently no real field for psychology. For, in these circumstances, if one wished to understand mental phenomena and the ways in which they reproduce and modify each other, one would not study them in themselves, but rather the anatomical conditions of which they are the more or less faithful reflections. We could not even say that they react upon and mutually modify each other, since these relations are only apparent. When we say of reflections in a mirror that they attract, repel, or succeed each other, etc., we accept these terms as metaphorical—we do not ascribe actual life to these movements. So little importance is attributed to these manifestations that we do not even wonder about their processes and disappearance. It is apparently quite natural that an idea which preoccupied us at one moment should cease to exist the next; it can only have seemed to exist if it can so easily vanish.

If the memory is solely a property of the tissues there is no mental life, for the mind does not exist outside the memory. This is not to say that intellectual activity is only the reproduction of earlier states of mind, but that for those states of mind to undergo an intellectual elaboration different from that implied in the laws of living matter they would have to have an existence relatively independent of their physical substratum. Otherwise they would be grouped as they are born and reborn, according to purely physical affinities. Some have tried to find an escape from this intellectual nihilism by imagining some sort of essence superior to phenomenal determinations. People talk vaguely of a mind which is distinct from the materials furnished by the brain and which elaborates them by *sui generis* processes. But what else is a mind that is not a system and sequence of particular thoughts but a hypostatized abstraction? Whether they exist or not, science is not concerned with essences or pure forms. For a psychologist the phenomenon of representation is only an assembly of representations. If these representations die as soon as they are born, then in what does the mind consist? We must choose: either epiphenomenalism is correct or else there is a memory that is a specifically mental phenomenon. But we have already seen that the first position is untenable, and consequently the second solution must be accepted if we are to remain consistent.

2

But we are forced to this conclusion for another reason. We have seen that, if the memory is exclusively one of the properties of neural matter, ideas have no power of mutual evocation; the order in which they occur to the mind can only reproduce the order in which their physical antecedents are restimulated, and this can be done only by physical causes. This proposition is so clearly implied in the premises of the theory that it is formally admitted by its adherents. It is a proposition that makes any psychic activity an abstraction lacking any reality, and it is directly contradicted by the facts. There are cases—and important ones—when the sequence of ideas does not appear to be explicable by such a theory. It is understandable, no doubt, that two ideas cannot appear together or follow each other immediately unless their substrata in the brain have some material connexion. Consequently there is no *a priori* impossibility in the restimulation of the one, following the line of least resistance, being spread to the other and thus determining the reappearance of its psychic manifestation. But there are no organic connexions known that can explain in what way one idea can evoke a similar idea simply because of their similarity. Nothing that we know about the brain leads us to suppose that a vibration at *A* will tend to spread to *B* simply because there is a similarity between the representations *a* and *b*. For this reason any psychology that sees the memory as a purely biological fact is unable to explain associations of resemblance except by reducing them to associations of contiguity—that is to say, by denying them all reality.

This has been in fact attempted.[1] It is argued that if two thoughts are similar they must have at least one element in common, and this identically repeated feature has in both cases the same neural element for support. This element is thus related to the two different groups of cells that correspond to the parts of the two representations that differ, since it has co-operated with both. Consequently it acts as a link between them, and thus the ideas are linked. If, for example, I see a piece of white paper the idea I carry away includes the impression of whiteness. The stimulation of the particular cell responsible for that colour induces a nervous current which will radiate round but which will tend to follow the paths to which it is habituated. That is to say, it will spread to those points that have previously been in communication with the first. But only those will satisfy this condition that have produced representations similar in this one respect with the first. Thus it is that the whiteness of the paper makes me think of the whiteness of snow. Thus two similar ideas are associated, but the association depends not upon similarity but solely upon the material contiguity.

This explanation rests on a series of arbitrary postulates. First of all, there is no justification for the supposition that representations are formed of definite elements or atoms that without losing their individuality go to the making up of various different representations. Ideas are not made up of bits and pieces which they exchange according to circumstances. The whiteness of paper is not the same as that of snow and the two appear in different representations. Will it be said that they both depend upon the general impression of whiteness which is common to both? If so, we should have to admit that the impression of white-

---

[1] The reference is to James, *Principles of Psychology*, I, p. 690. There is no p. 690. The reader is referred to chapters xiv and xvi, which deal respectively with Association and Memory.—D. F. P.

ness in general constitutes a sort of distinct entity which, grouped with other entities, gives birth to a particular sensation of whiteness. However, there are no facts to justify such an hypothesis. Everything goes to show that, on the contrary—and it is interesting that James has contributed more than anyone in drawing attention to the proposition—psychic existence is a continual stream of representations that blend into each other so that no one can say where one begins or another finishes. No doubt the intellect comes to make certain divisions, but it is we who introduce them into the psychic *continuum*. This process of abstraction allows us to analyse what is, in fact, an indivisible complex. According to the hypothesis which we have just discussed the brain could make these analyses itself, since these divisions would have an anatomical basis. We know the difficulty we meet with when we try to give the products of abstraction some sort of precarious form and individuality by the use of language, quite apart from entertaining the supposition that this dissociation corresponds to the original nature of the facts!

The physiological assumptions at the base of the theory are even more questionable. If we concede that ideas can be decomposed into parts, we should have to admit further that to each of the parts corresponds a particular neural element. Thus we should have one part of the cerebral mass devoted to sensations of red, another to sensations of green, etc. Even this would not be enough, for there would have to be particular substrata for each shade of green, red, etc. For according to the hypothesis two colours of the same shade cannot evoke each other unless their point of resemblance corresponds to one and the same organic point, since all psychic similarity implies spatial coincidence. Such a geography of the brain belongs to the world of the novelette rather than to that of science. No doubt we know that certain intellectual functions are more closely bound to certain regions than to others, but that these localizations are in no way precise or rigorous is demonstrated by the phenomenon of substitution. To go further and to suppose that each representation dwells in a particular cell is a gratuitous postulate, and one which the conclusion of this study will demonstrate to be impossible. What is to be said in favour of the hypothesis that maintains that each of the finest elements of the representation (allowing for the moment that they exist) is no less narrowly localized? Thus the representation of the paper on which I am now writing is literally scattered throughout the recesses of my brain. There must not only be a place for the impression of colour, for the form and the texture, but the idea of the colour in general will be in one place, the particular shade in another, and elsewhere the special characteristics which this shade takes on in the present individual case when it is before my eyes, etc. Surely it can be seen, quite apart from any other consideration, that if mental life is divided to this degree and made up of these myriads of organic elements, the unity and continuity which it presents are incomprehensible?

We could also ask how it comes about, if the resemblance of two representations is due to the presence of one and the same element in both, that this element appears as doubled. If we have an image ABCD, and another AEFG evoked by the first, and if consequently the total process may be formulated as (BCD) A (EFG), then how is it that we see two A's? It will be argued that this distinction arises as a result of the differential elements given at the same time: as A is involved at one and the same time with the complex BCD and the complex EFG, and as these complexes are distinct from each other, logically we are bound to admit that A has been doubled. This, however, only explains why we are bound to *postulate* this duality; it does not for all that explain why it is, in fact, that we *see* it. While we may conjecture that one image is related to two different complexes of circumstances, it does not follow that we should *see it doubled*. At this very moment, let us suppose, I have before my eyes on the one hand this piece of white paper and on the other the snow outside on the ground. There are in my mind two representations of whiteness and not one only. To reduce similarity to a partial identity is to make an artificial simplification. Two similar ideas are distinct, even in those aspects which constitute the similarity. The elements which they are said to have in common are separate in the one and in the other; we do not confuse them even while we compare them. It is the *sui generis* relationship which is established between them, the special combination which they form by virtue of this resemblance, the particular characteristics of this combination, which give us the impression of similarity; combination presupposes plurality.

One cannot then reduce resemblance to contiguity without mistaking the nature of resemblance and forming hypotheses, at the same time physiological and psychological, which cannot be justified; from this it follows that the memory is not a purely physical fact and that representations as such have permanence. If, in fact, they vanished entirely as soon as they had left the present consciousness, if they only survived as organic impressions, the similarity which they might have with a particular present idea would not suffice to bring them to life again, since no relationship of similarity can exist either directly or indirectly between this surviving physical trace and a presently existing mental condition. If at the moment that I see this piece of paper there exists in my mind nothing of the snow which I saw previously, the first image cannot work upon the second nor the second on the first; the one cannot evoke the other by the mere fact of similarity. The phenomenon is, however, no longer unintelligible if the memory is a mental fact, if past representations exist as such and if the act of remembering consists, not in a new and original creation, but in a new emergence into the light of consciousness. If our psychic life is not annihilated at the same time that it unfolds, if there is no solution of continuity between our earlier and our present states of mind, then there is no impossibility in the proposition that they can work upon each other and that the result of this mutual action can, in certain conditions, so increase the intensity of the earlier ones that they come once again to consciousness.

It has been objected, it is true, that resemblance cannot explain association of ideas, since it cannot appear until ideas have already been associated. It is argued that resemblance is recognized because the ideas in question have become associated and therefore cannot be the cause of this relationship. But this argument confuses resemblance itself with the perception of that resemblance. Two representations can be similar, as the things which they express, without our knowing it. The principal discoveries of science consist precisely in this perception of previously unnoted analogies between ideas that are known to everyone. Why should not this unperceived resemblance not produce effects which would serve to characterize it and make it apparent? Images and ideas work upon each other and these actions and reactions must necessarily vary with the nature of the representations; particularly they must change according as the representations which are in this manner brought together resemble each other, differ or contrast. There is no reason why resemblance should not develop a *sui generis* property by virtue of which two conditions separated by an interval of time should be made to come together. In order to admit this as a reality it is not at all necessary to imagine representations as things having a separate existence; it is merely sufficient to admit that they are not non-entities, that they are phenomena but endowed with reality, with specific properties which behave in different ways with each other according as they have, or have not, common properties. One could find in the natural sciences many examples of the same thing. When bodies of different densities are mingled those with a similar density tend to group together and separate themselves from the others. Among living things similar elements have such an affinity that they tend to lose themselves in fusion and become indistinct. Certainly this phenomenon of attraction and coalescence can be explained by mechanical reasons and not by a mysterious attraction which like has for like. But why cannot the grouping of similar representations in the mind be explained in an analogous manner? Why should there not be a mental mechanism (not exclusively physical) which should explain these associations without introducing any occult faculty or scholastic entity?

Even at the present stage of knowledge it is possible to see roughly the path along which such an inquiry would be guided. A representation does not appear without affecting the body and mind. The very fact of its birth presupposes certain movements. In order to see a house which is in front of me, I have to contract the muscles of the eye in a particular manner and incline the head according to the height and dimensions of the building; furthermore, the sensation, once it exists, in its turn determines certain movements. Now if this has already happened once, if that is, the same house has been seen before, the same movements were performed. The same muscles were moved, and in the same manner to a certain extent, in so far, that is, as the subjective and objective conditions of the experience are repeated identically. There exists, then, a definite connexion between the image of this house in my memory and certain movements. Since these movements are the same as those which accompany my present sensation of the house, through them is established a link between my present and my past perception. Brought into being by the first they reawaken the second; it is a well-known fact that by arranging the body in a particular attitude one can evoke the corresponding ideas or emotions.

Nevertheless, this first factor is not the most important. However real the relation between ideas and movements may be, it is not at all precise. The same system of movements can serve very different ideas without being modified proportionately, and also the ideas which are thus evoked are always of the most general kind. By arranging the subject's limbs in a suitable position one can suggest the idea of prayer in general but not of a particular prayer. If it is true that any condition of the mind is involved with movement, it must be added that, the further representations are from pure sensation, the more the element of movement loses its importance and positive significance. The superior intellectual functions presuppose the inhibition of movement, as is proved by the predominant role played among them by concentration and the nature of concentration itself, which consists in as complete a suspension as is possible of all physical activity. However, a simple denial of the faculty of movement does not suffice to characterize the infinite diversity of the phenomena of ideation. The effort which we make to refrain from action is no more bound to this conception than to another, if the second has exacted of us the same degree of attention as the first. But the link between the present and the past can also be established with the help of purely intellectual intermediaries. All representations from the moment that they come into being affect, apart from the organs, the mind itself. That is to say, they affect the present and past representations which constitute the mind, if it is admitted that past representations *do* persist·with us. The picture which I see at a given moment reacts upon my manner of seeing, my aspirations and desires. My sight of this picture is then, in a sense, responsible for these diverse mental elements. If I see the picture again it will act in the same way on these same elements, which persist unchanged except for the modifications which time has perhaps brought about. It will excite them as it did on the first occasion, and through them this stimulus will be communicated to the previous representation with which, from now onwards, they are related and which is thus revived. For unless we are to deny to psychic conditions all effective force, there is no reason why they should not be able to transmit their energy to the mental conditions with which they are related, just as the movement in one cell can be transmitted to neighbouring cells. As regards representational life, these phenomena of transference make it all the more easy to conceive that it is not formed of separate and distinct atoms but is a continuous whole of interpenetrating parts.

We offer the reader this sketchy explanation only as an indication. Our aim is above all to demonstrate that there is no impossibility in resemblance being in itself the cause of association. It has so often been argued that the so-called impossibility of this makes it necessary to reduce similarity to contiguity and mental memory to physical memory, that it seemed to us important to show that this original difficulty was by no means an insuperable one.

3

Thus not only is the concession that representations can persist as such the sole means of escape from an epiphenomenalist psychology, but also the existence of the association of ideas by resemblance demonstrates this persistence.

It has, however, been claimed that these difficulties have been escaped only at the price of incurring a greater. It is argued that if representations can persist as such they must do so outside the consciousness, for we have no conception of all the ideas, sensations, etc., which we have experienced in the past and which we are likely to remember in the future. If consciousness is implicit in the nature of representation, then one must conclude that the idea of an unconscious representation is inconceivable and a contradiction in terms.

But by what right do we thus limit the psychic life? If the argument is only over words, it is perhaps legitimate but scarcely fruitful. Because it is convenient to call the conscious states of mind psychological it does not follow that outside consciousness there are only organic or bio-chemical phenomena. It is a question of fact which only observation can answer. Would it be argued that, if one were to withdraw consciousness from representation, what remains would be incapable of representation to the imagination? But in this way there are thousands of authentic facts which could equally well be denied. We do not know what an imponderable material environment is, nor can we conceive an idea of it; nevertheless the hypothesis is necessary for the explanation of the transmission of light waves. How many well-established cases suggest that thought can travel over a distance? The difficulty which we may have in conceiving so disconcerting an idea is not sufficient reason for us to deny its reality, and we shall in all probability have to admit the existence of waves of thought: a notion which is beyond, and even contradicts, our present conceptions. Before the existence of invisible light rays able to pierce opaque bodies was demonstrated, it had been easily proved that they were irreconcilable with the nature of light. One could multiply these examples. Because, then, a phenomenon is not easily presented to the mind, that is no justification for denying its existence when it manifests itself in definite effects which are representable and which serve it in the capacity of signs. Such phenomena are thought of, not in themselves, but by the effects which characterize them. There is not a science that has not been forced to make this detour in order to arrive at the facts it studies. Science goes from without, from the external and immediately sensible manifestations, to the interior characteristics of which these manifestations betray the existence. A nervous current or a light ray is, to begin with, an unknown quantity recognized as present by this or that particular effect, and the task of a science is precisely to determine the exact content of this initial conception. If, then, we are forced to say that certain phenomena can only be caused by representations, that these phenomena are the outward signs of representational life, and if, on the other hand, the subject in whom these representations appear is ignorant of them, we shall say that unconscious psychic states can exist, however hard it may be for the imagination to conceive their existence.

Instances of this are innumerable if, at least, we understand by consciousness the apprehension of a given state by a given subject. In fact, within each one of us a multitude of psychic phenomena occur without our apprehending them. We say that they are psychic because they make themselves apparent by their characteristic signs of mental activity, recognized by hesitation, tentativeness and the adjustment of movement to a preconceived end. If when an act directed towards a particular goal takes place we are not sure that it is intelligent, one wonders by what faculty the intelligence is able to distinguish itself from what is not itself. The experiments of M. Pierre Janet have proved that many acts, while bearing all the signs of being conscious, are not in fact so. For example, a subject who had just refused to execute an order complies docilely when his attention is distracted just at the moment when the words of command are given. It is evidently a complex of representations which dictates his attitude, for the order cannot have its effect unless it has been heard and understood. However, the patient does not know what is going on, he does not even know that he has obeyed. If at the moment when he is about to perform the required gesture his action is pointed out to him, it is, for him, the most surprising discovery.[1] In the same way, when one forbids a hypnotized subject to see a person or object in front of him, the order will have effect only if it is impressed upon the mind. Nevertheless the consciousness is not aware of it. There are cases also of unconscious counting and complex calculations performed by an individual who had no idea

[1] See Janet, *L'Automatisme psychologique*, p. 237 et seq. [See also, for James's discussion of Janet, James, op. cit., I, pp. 203 et seq. For James's discussion of the question 'Can states of mind be unconscious?' see op. cit., I, pp. 162 et seq. D.F.P.]

of what he was doing.[1] These experiments, which have been varied, have, it is true, been conducted with abnormal subjects, but they only reproduced in amplified form what normally occurs in all of us. Our judgments are influenced at every moment by unconscious judgments; we see only what our prejudices permit us to see and yet we are unaware of them. We are always to a certain extent in a state of distraction, since the attention, in concentrating the mind upon a small number of objects, blinds it to a greater number of others; all distraction has the effect of withdrawing certain psychic states from consciousness which do not cease to be real for all that, since they continue to function. How many times is there a positive contradiction between the actual state of a thing as it is and as it appears in the mind? We imagine that we hate someone when in fact we love him, and the reality of this love shows itself in acts that are apparent to others while we believe ourselves to be under the influence of completely opposite sentiments.[2]

Furthermore, if all that is psychic were conscious, and all that is unconscious physiological, psychology would return to the old method of introspection. For if the reality of mental states is the same as our consciousness of them, the conscious mind would suffice for the complete under-

[1] Janet, ibid., p. 225.

[2] According to James this is no proof of lack of consciousness. If I imagine that I hate or am indifferent when in fact I am in love, I have merely misnamed a condition of which I am fully conscious. I must confess that I do not understand this. If I misname a condition, it is because my consciousness of it also is false and does not express all the characteristics of this condition. Nevertheless these characteristics which are not conscious still function. They are then, in a way, unconscious. My feelings have all the constituent traits of love since they affect my conduct; but I do not recognize them, so that in a sense my passions direct me one way and the knowledge which I have of them, another. The two phenomena are not coterminous. Nevertheless it is difficult to see in an inclination like love anything other than a psychic phenomenon. (See James, op. cit., I, p. 174.)

5

standing of this reality, since they would be the same thing, and there would be no need for recourse to the complicated and roundabout methods at present in use. We can, in fact, no longer regard the laws of phenomena as superior to the phenomena and directing them from without. The laws are immanent in them and are their manner of being. If, then, mental facts are only as we see them and only act as we are conscious of them acting (which is the same thing), their laws are given at the same time. In order to understand them we have only to look at them. As for those factors of mental life which are unconscious and consequently cannot be studied in this way, they will have to come within the field not of psychology but of physiology. There is no need for us to demonstrate the fallacy of so facile a psychology; there is no question that the interior world of the mind is still, to a great extent, unexplored; that discoveries are constantly being made and many more are yet to be made and that, consequently, it will call for more than a little application of the conscious mind to make them. It is useless to argue that those representations that pass for unconscious are only perceived incompletely and confusedly; for this confusion can have only one cause, simply that we do not see all that these representations comprehend—that there are *real and effective* elements which are not, consequently, purely physical facts, and which are not, however, obvious to the consciousness. This obscure consciousness is a partial unconsciousness, and we must once again remember that the limits of consciousness are not the limits of all psychic activity.

In order to avoid this word 'unconscious' and the attendant difficulties which the mind faces in conceiving its content, one might say that unconscious phenomena are attached to centres of secondary consciousness dispersed throughout the organism and unknown to the primary centre, while normally subordinate to it. Also one could say that consciousness can exist without any apprehension by a given subject's *ego*. We cannot at the moment discuss these hypotheses[1] which, although plausible, leave un-assailed the proposition which we wish to establish. All that we wish to say is that certain phenomena occur in us which are of a psychic order and which are nevertheless not known by our conscious selves. Whether they are known to some other unknown 'self' or whether they are outside the realm of all apprehension is not for us a matter of primary importance. All we wish to be conceded is that representational life extends beyond our present conscious-ness and, as a consequence, that the conception of memory as a fact of the psychological order is an intelligible pro-position. All that we are trying to make clear here is that such a memory exists without going into all the possible ways in which it can be conceived.

4

We are now in a position to conclude.

If representations, once they exist, continue to exist in *themselves* without their existence being perpetually de-pendent upon the disposition of the neural centres, if they have the power to react directly upon each other and to combine according to their own laws, they are then realities which, while maintaining an intimate relation with their substratum, are to a certain extent independent of it. Certainly their autonomy can only be a relative one; there is no realm of nature that is not bound to others. Nothing could be more absurd than to elevate psychic life into a sort of absolute, derived from nothing and unattached to the rest of the universe. It is obvious that the condition

[1] The idea of an unconscious representation and that of a con-sciousness without the *ego* are basically equivalent. When we say a mental fact is unconscious we mean simply that it is not apprehended. The question is merely which is the more suitable expression. From the point of view of the imagination both are equally difficult. It is no easier for us to imagine a representation without the thinking subject than to imagine a representation without consciousness.

of the brain affects all the intellectual phenomena and is the immediate cause of some of them (pure sensation). But, on the other hand, it follows from what has been said earlier that representational life is not inherent in the intrinsic nature of nervous matter, since in part it exists by its own force and has its own particular manner of being. A representation is not simply an aspect of the condition of a neural element at the particular moment that it takes place, since it persists after that condition has passed, and since the relations of the representations are different in nature from those of the underlying neural elements. It is something quite new which certain characteristics of the cells certainly help to produce but do not suffice to constitute, since it survives them and manifests different properties. To say that the mental condition does not derive directly from the cell is to say that it is not included in it, that it forms itself in part outside it and is to that extent exterior to it. If it was directly derived it would be within it, since its reality would derive from no other source.

When we said elsewhere that social facts are in a sense independent of individuals and exterior to individual minds, we only affirmed of the social world what we have just established for the psychic world. Society has for its substratum the mass of associated individuals. The system which they form by uniting together, and which varies according to their geographical disposition and the nature and number of their channels of communication, is the base from which social life is raised. The representations which form the network of social life arise from the relations between the individuals thus combined or the secondary groups that are between the individuals and the total society. If there is nothing extraordinary in the fact that individual representations, produced by the action and reaction between neural elements, are not inherent in these elements, there is nothing surprising in the fact that collective representations, produced by the action and reaction between individual minds that form the society, do not derive directly from the latter and consequently surpass them. The conception of the relationship which unites the social substratum and the social life is at every point analogous to that which undeniably exists between the physiological substratum and the psychic life of individuals, if, that is, one is not going to deny the existence of psychology in the proper sense of the word. The same consequences should then follow on both sides. The independence, the relative externality of social facts in relation to individuals, is even more immediately apparent than is that of mental facts in relation to the cerebral cells, for the former, or at least the most important of them, bear the clear marks of their origin. While one might perhaps contest the statement that all social facts without exception impose themselves from without upon the individual, the doubt does not seem possible as regards religious beliefs and practices, the rules of morality and the innumerable precepts of law—that is to say, all the most characteristic manifestations of collective life. All are expressly obligatory, and this obligation is the proof that these ways of acting and thinking are not the work of the individual but come from a moral power above him, that which the mystic calls God or which can be more scientifically conceived.[1] The same law is found at work in the two fields.

Furthermore, it can be explained in the same way in the two cases. If one can say that, to a certain extent, collective

---

[1] If the characteristics of obligation and constraint are so essential to these eminently social facts, it is to be expected that they will be found, if less obviously, in other social facts. It is impossible for phenomena of the same nature to differ to the extent that some penetrate to the individual from without and others are the result of a different process.

We should like here to correct a false interpretation that has been put upon our thought. When we said that obligation and constraint are the characteristics of social facts we had no intention of giving a summary explanation of the latter. We wished simply to point out a convenient sign by which the sociologist can recognize the facts falling within his field.

representations are exterior to individual minds, it means that they do not derive from them as such but from the association of minds, which is a very different thing. No doubt in the making of the whole each contributes his part, but private sentiments do not become social except by combination under the action of the *sui generis* forces developed in association. In such a combination, with the mutual alterations involved, *they become something else.* A chemical synthesis results which concentrates and unifies the synthesised elements and by that transforms them. Since this synthesis is the work of the whole, its sphere is the whole. The resultant surpasses the individual as the whole the part. It is *in* the whole as it is *by* the whole. In this sense it is exterior to the individuals. No doubt each individual contains a part, but the whole is found in no one. In order to understand it as it is one must take the aggregate in its totality into consideration.[1] It is that which thinks, feels, wishes, even though it can neither wish, feel, nor act except through individual minds. We can see here also how it is that society does not depend upon the nature of the individual personality. In the fusion from which it results all the individual characteristics, by definition divergent, have neutralized each other. Only those more general properties of human nature survive, and precisely because of their extreme generality they cannot account for the specialized and complex forms which characterize collective facts. This is not to say that they count for nothing in the resultant, but they are only its mediate conditions. Without them it could not emerge, but they do not determine it.

The exteriority of mental facts in relation to the cerebral cells is due to the same causes and is of the same nature. Nothing, in fact, justifies the supposition that any representation, however elementary, can be directly produced by a cellular vibration of a given intensity and tone. But there is no sensation which is unrelated to a certain number of

[1] See *Le Suicide,* pp. 345-63.

cells. The manner of cerebral localizations admits of no other hypothesis, for the images are definitely related only to more or less extended zones. Perhaps, as the fact of substitutions seems to show, the whole brain participates in the elaboration from which they result. At least, this seems to be the only way in which we can explain how it is that sensation is dependent upon the brain while at the same time constituting a new phenomenon. It is dependent because it is formed as a result of molecular modifications; how could it be made otherwise and whence could it derive? But it is at the same time another thing because it results from a new and *sui generis* synthesis into which these modifications enter as elements, but in which they are transformed by the very fact of their fusion. Certainly we do not know exactly how these combined movements do give rise to a representation, but neither do we know how it is that movement can be translated into heat by being arrested in its course or how heat is translated into movement. However, there is no doubt about the transformation itself; what then is there more impossible about the first? More generally this objection would strike at the root of all change, for between 'an effect and its causes, a resultant and its elements, there is always a qualitative distance (*écart*). It is for metaphysics to find the concepts which will render this heterogeneity in an acceptable form; for us it is sufficient that its existence cannot be contested.

But if each idea (or at least each sensation) is due to the synthesis of a number of cellular conditions, combined according to laws by forces which we do not as yet know, it is obvious that it cannot be limited to one particular cell. It escapes from each because none is sufficient of itself to bring it into being. Representational life cannot be divided among and ascribed to particular neural elements, since several of these elements combine for its generation; *but it could not exist without the whole formed by their union, just as the collective could not exist without the whole formed by the union of individuals.* Neither the one nor the other is made up of particular parts that can be attributed to the corresponding parts of their respective substrata. Each mental condition is, as regards the neural cells, in the same condition of relative independence as social phenomena are in relation to individual people. As it cannot be reduced to a simple molecular modification it is not subject to modifications of this kind, which can happen in isolation at different points in the brain. Only those physical forces that affect the entire group of cells that support it can affect it also. But in order to survive, it is not in need of constant support and, as it were, constant recreation by a continuous stream of nervous energy. To recognize this limited autonomy of the mind is basically the same as the essential and positive content of our notion of *spirituality*. There is no need to conceive of a soul separated from its body maintaining in some ideal milieu a dreamy and solitary existence. The soul is in the world and its life is involved with the life of things, or we could say that all our thoughts are in the brain. We must add that within the brain, while they may be more related to certain areas of it than to others, they cannot be rigidly localized or situated at definite points. This diffusion in itself is sufficient proof that they constitute a specifically new phenomenon. In order that this diffusion can exist, their composition must be different from that of the cerebral mass, and consequently they must have a manner of being which is special to them.

Those, then, who accuse us of leaving social life in the air because we refuse to reduce it to the individual mind have not, perhaps, recognized all the consequences of their objection. If it were justified it would apply just as well to the relations between mind and brain, for in order to be logical they must reduce the mind to the cell and deny mental life all specificity. But then one falls into the dire difficulties that we have already indicated. Following the same principle, one would be bound to say that the properties of life consist in particles of oxygen, hydrogen, carbon and nitrogen, which compose the living protoplasm, since it contains nothing beyond these particular minerals just as society contains nothing more than the individuals.[1] Here the impossibility of the conception which we are opposing will perhaps appear with even greater clarity than in the earlier instances. How can living movements be based in non-living elements? How are the characteristic properties of life distributed among these elements? They cannot be equally divided since they are different. Oxygen cannot play the same role as carbon or be invested with the same properties. No less inadmissible is the contention that each aspect of life is embodied in a different group of atoms. Life cannot be thus divided; it is one, and consequently cannot be based on anything other than the living substance in its totality. It is in the whole, not in the parts. If, then, to understand it as it is, it is not necessary to disperse it among the elementary forces of which it is the resultant, why should it be different for the individual mind in relation to the cerebral cells and social facts in relation to individuals?

In fact individualistic sociology is only applying the old principles of materialist metaphysics to social life. It claims, that is, to explain the complex by the simple, the superior by the inferior, and the whole by the part, which is a contradiction in terms. The contrary principle does not seem to us to be any less questionable. One cannot, following idealist and theological metaphysics, derive the part from the whole, since the whole is nothing without the parts which form it and cannot draw its vital necessities from the void. We must, then, explain phenomena that are the product of the whole by the characteristic properties of the whole, the complex by the complex, social facts by society, vital and mental facts by the *sui generis* combinations from which they result. This is the only path that a science can follow. This is not to say that there is a solution of continuity between these various

[1] At least, individuals are the only active elements. More correctly, society also comprises things.

stages of reality. The whole is only formed by the grouping of the parts, and this grouping does not take place suddenly as a result of a miracle. There is an infinite series of intermediaries between the state of pure isolation and the completed state of association. But as the association is formed it gives birth to phenomena which do not derive directly from the nature of the associated elements, and the more elements involved and the more powerful their synthesis, then the more marked is this partial independence. No doubt it is this that accounts for the flexibility, freedom and contingence that the superior forms of reality show in comparison with the lower forms in which they are rooted. In fact, when a way of doing or being depends from a whole without depending immediately from the parts which compose that whole, it enjoys, as a result of this diffusion, a ubiquity which to a certain extent frees it. As it is not fixed to a particular point in space it is not bound by too narrowly limited conditions of existence. If some cause induces a variation, that variation will encounter less resistance and will come into existence more easily because it has, in a way, a greater scope for movement. If certain of the parts reject it, certain others will form the basis (*point d'appui*) necessary for the new arrangement without, for all that, being obliged to rearrange themselves. That at least is how one can conceive how it is that one organ is able to perform different functions, different parts of the brain can substitute for each other, and one social institution can successively further the most varied ends.

Also, while it is through the collective substratum that collective life is connected to the rest of the world, it is not absorbed in it. It is at the same time dependent on and distinct from it, as is the function of the organ. As it is born of the collective substratum the forms which it manifests at the time of its origin, and which are consequently fundamental, naturally bear the marks of their origin. For this reason the basic matter of the social consciousness is in close relation with the number of social elements and the way in which they are grouped and distributed, etc.— that is to say, with the nature of the substratum. But once a basic number of representations has been thus created, they become, for the reasons which we have explained, partially autonomous realities with their own way of life. They have the power to attract and repel each other and to form amongst themselves various syntheses, which are determined by their natural affinities and not by the condition of their matrix. As a consequence, the new representations born of these syntheses have the same nature; they are immediately caused by other collective representations and not by this or that characteristic of the social structure. The evolution of religion provides us with the most striking examples of this phenomenon. It is perhaps impossible to understand how the Greek or Roman Pantheon came into existence unless we go into the constitution of the city, the way in which the primitive clans slowly merged, the organization of the patriarchal family, etc. Nevertheless the luxuriant growth of myths and legends, theogonic and cosmological systems, etc., which grow out of religious thought, is not directly related to the particular features of the social morphology. Thus it is that the social nature of religion has been so often misunderstood.

It has been believed that it is formed to a great extent by extra-social forces because the immediate link between the greater part of religious beliefs and the organization of society has not been perceived. By this reasoning one would have to exclude from psychology everything beyond pure sensation. For if sensation, this primary store of the individual mind, cannot be explained except by the condition of the brain and the organs, once it exists it forms itself according to laws which neither morphology nor cerebral physiology can adequately account for. From this derive images and these, in their turn, group to form conceptions. As these new states are added to the old, as they are separated by more intermediaries from the organic base upon which, nevertheless, all mental life rests, they become less immediately dependent upon it. They do not cease to be psychic facts, for it is in them that one can best observe the characteristic attributes of the mind.[1]

Perhaps these comparisons will make clear why we insist so much upon a distinction between sociology and individual psychology.

It is simply a matter of introducing and acclimatizing in sociology a conception parallel to that which is tending to prevail more and more in psychology. During the last decade a great innovation has been made in that science. Interesting efforts have been made to establish a psychology which is in fact psychological without any other qualifying adjective. The old introspectionists were content to describe mental phenomena without trying to explain them; psycho-physiology explained them but dismissed their distinctive traits as negligible. A third school is being born which is trying to explain them without destroying

[1] From this it can be seen how difficult it is to define social facts as phenomena produced *in* but also *by* the society. The expression is not exact, for there are social facts, and not among the least, which are produced, not by the society but by already formed social products. It is as though one were to define as mental facts those which are the product of the combined action of the cerebral cells or a certain number of them. Such a definition will not serve to determine and circumscribe the object of sociology. The relation of these derivatives can only be established as the science advances. At the beginning of research one does not know the causes of the phenomena that are being studied, and indeed one can only hope to know little. We must then limit the field of investigation by another criterion if we wish to know clearly what we are concerned with.

The process by which these social products of the second degree are formed, if analogous with that observed in the individual mind, is also an individual phenomenon. The combinations from which myths, theogonies and popular cosmogonies result are not identical with the association of ideas in the individual mind, even though each throws some light on the other. A special branch of sociology, which does not yet exist, should be devoted to research into the laws of collective ideation.

their specificity. For the first mental life certainly had a nature of its own, but it was one that lifted the mental out of the world and above the ordinary methods of science. For the second school it was nothing in itself, and the role of the scientist was to pierce the superficial stratum in order to arrive at the underlying realities. Neither school saw anything more than a thin curtain of phenomena which, according to the first, was easily apparent to the eye of the conscious mind and, to the second, was lacking in any consistency. Recent experiments have shown us that it is far better to conceive of it as a vast system of *sui generis* realities made up of a great number of mental strata superimposed upon each other, far too profound and complex for the conscious mind to pierce, far too specialized to be accounted for by purely physiological considerations. It is thus that this *spirituality* by which we characterize intellectual facts, and which seemed in the past to be either above or below the attentions of science, has become itself the object of a positive science, and that, between the ideology of the introspectionists and biological naturalism, a psychological naturalism has been founded, the legitimacy of which the present article will, perhaps, help to demonstrate.

A similar transformation should take place in sociology, and it is towards this goal that all our efforts are directed. If there are no longer many thinkers who dare explicitly to put social facts beyond the realm of nature, many still think that it is sufficient in order to explain them to go to the individual mind; certain others even wish to reduce them to the general properties of organic matter. For all of them, consequently, society is nothing in itself; it is only an epiphenomenon of individual life (organic or mental, it makes no difference) just as, according to Maudsley and his disciples, individual representation is only an epiphenomenon of physical life. The first would have no other reality than that which it received from the individual, just as the second would have no other existence than that which it takes from the neural cell, and sociology would become applied psychology.[1] But even the example of psychology shows that this conception of science should be discarded. Beyond the ideology of the psycho-sociologist and the materialistic naturalism of the socio-anthropologist there is room for a sociological naturalism which would see in social phenomena specific facts, and which would undertake to explain them while preserving a religious respect for their specificity. Nothing is wider of the mark than the mistaken accusation of materialism which has been levelled against us. Quite the contrary: from the point of view of our position, if one is to call the distinctive property of the individual representational life *spirituality*, one should say that social life is defined by its *hyper-spirituality*. By this we mean that all the constituent attributes of mental life are found in it, but elevated to a very much higher power and in such a manner as to constitute something entirely new. Despite its metaphysical appearance, this word designates nothing more than a body of natural facts which are explained by natural causes. It does, however, warn us that the new world thus opened to science surpasses all others in complexity; it is not merely a lower field of study conceived in more ambitious terms, but one in which as yet unsuspected forces are at work, and of which the laws may not be discovered by the methods of interior analysis alone.

[1] When we use the word 'psychology' by itself we mean individual psychology, and for the sake of clarity in discussion it is convenient to limit the word to this. Collective psychology is sociology, quite simply —why not employ the latter term exclusively? Inversely the word 'psychology' has always designated the science of the individual mentality—why not reserve this meaning to it? Thus we should avoid much ambiguity.

II

THE DETERMINATION OF MORAL FACTS[1]

THESES

MORAL reality, like all reality, can be studied from two different points of view. One can set out to explore and understand it and one can set out to evaluate it. The first of these problems, which is theoretical, must necessarily precede the second, and it is the only one with which we shall deal here. In closing, however, we shall show that the methods followed and the solutions adopted leave the field clear for the treatment of the practical problem.

For the theoretical study of moral reality we must determine beforehand the nature of moral facts. In order to observe them we must know their characteristics so that we can recognize them. This is the first question we shall deal with. Later we shall see if it is possible to give a satisfactory explanation of these characteristics.

I

What are the distinctive characteristics of a moral fact?

All morality appears to us as a system of rules of conduct. But all techniques are equally ruled by maxims that prescribe the behaviour of the agent in particular circumstances. What then is the difference between moral rules and other rules of technique?

(i) We shall show that moral rules are invested with a

---

[1] Extract from the *Bulletin de la Société Française de Philosophie*. The theses reproduced here were distributed to the members by Durkheim. They are followed by part of his discussion of these theses at the seminar which took place on 11 February, 1906.

special authority by virtue of which they are obeyed simply because they command. We shall reaffirm, as a result of a purely empirical analysis, the notion of duty and nevertheless give a definition of it closely resembling that already given by Kant. Obligation is, then, one of the primary characteristics of the moral rule.

(ii) In opposition to Kant, however, we shall show that the notion of duty does not exhaust the concept of morality. It is impossible for us to carry out an act simply because we are ordered to do so and without consideration of its content. For us to become the agents of an act it must interest our sensibility to a certain extent and appear to us as, in some way, *desirable*. Obligation or duty only expresses one aspect abstracted from morality. A certain degree of desirability is another characteristic no less important than the first.

Something of the nature of duty is found in the desirability of morality. If it is true that the content of the act appeals to us, nevertheless its nature is such that it cannot be accomplished without effort and self-constraint. The *élan*, even the enthusiasm, with which we perform a moral act takes us outside ourselves and above our nature, and this is not achieved without difficulty and inner conflict. It is this *sui generis* desirability which is commonly called *good*.

Desirability and obligation are the two characteristics which it is useful to stress, without necessarily denying the existence of others. It will be our main intention to show that all moral acts have these two characteristics, even though they may be combined in different proportions.

In order to give some idea of these two partly contradictory aspects of moral facts, we shall compare them to the idea of *sacredness*, which has the same duality. The sacred being is in a sense forbidden; it is a being which may not be violated; it is also good, loved and sought after. The association of these two qualities will be justified: (i) historically by an examination of the filiation which links them; (ii) by examples taken from contemporary morality. The human personality is a sacred thing; one dare not violate it nor infringe its bounds, while at the same time the greatest good is in communion with others.

2

Having determined these characteristics, we should try to discover a means of understanding how it is that certain precepts are obeyed because they command, and also cause us to perform those acts which are desirable in the sense that we have noted above. A methodical reply to this question would call for as exhaustive a study as possible of the particular rules the sum total of which constitutes our morality. But instead of such a study, which is impossible in these circumstances, it is possible to use more summary means to arrive at results of some value.

By examining the contemporary moral consciousness (and checking our findings by what we know of the moralities of all known peoples) we can agree upon the following points: (i) The qualification 'moral' has never been given to an act which has individual interests, or the perfection of the individual from a purely egotistic point of view, as its object; (ii) if I as an individual do not constitute *in myself* a moral end, this is also true of the other individuals who are more or less like me; (iii) from which we conclude that, *if a morality exists*, it can only have as object the group formed by the associated individuals—that is to say, society, *with the condition that society be always considered as being qualitatively different from the individual beings that compose it*. Morality begins with membership of a group, whatever that group may be. When this premise is accepted the characteristics of the moral fact become explicable. First, we shall show how society is good and desirable for the individual who cannot exist without it or deny it without denying himself, and how at the same time, because society surpasses the individual, he cannot desire it without to a certain extent violating his nature as an individual.

Secondly, we shall show that society, while being good, constitutes a moral authority which, by manifesting itself in certain precepts particularly important to it, confers ·upon them an obligatory character.

We shall endeavour further to establish that certain ends —devotion between individuals, the devotion of a scientist to his work—which are not in themselves moral ends, participate of morality indirectly and by derivation.

Finally, an analysis of collective sentiments will explain the characteristic of *sacredness* which is attributed to moral facts; an analysis which will, however, only serve to confirm the preceding analysis.

3

The objection has been made to this conception that it subjugates the mind to the prevailing moral opinion. This is not so. The society that morality bids us desire is not the society as it *appears* to itself, but the society as it is or is really becoming. The consciousness which society may have of itself which is expressed in general opinion (*dans et par l'opinion*) may be an inadequate view of the underlying reality. It is possible that opinion, weighed down by survivals, lags behind the real condition of the society. It is also possible that, under the effect of passing circumstances, certain principles, even though essential to the existing morality, may for a time be relegated to the unconscious and so appear not to exist. The science of morality will allow us to rectify these errors, of which we shall later give examples.

But we shall maintain that it is impossible to desire a morality other than that endorsed by the condition of society at a given time. To desire a morality other than that implied by the nature of society is to deny the latter and, consequently, oneself.

The question remains: Should a man deny himself? This is a legitimate question, but we shall not examine it. We shall postulate that we are right in wishing to live.

Discussion

DURKHEIM: I must first of all confess briefly to a certain embarrassment. In agreeing to discuss *ex abrupto* a question as general as that announced in the second part of the programme[1] distributed to you, I am forced to do violence to my habitual methods of procedure. Certainly, in the course which I have been giving at the Sorbonne for four years upon the theoretical and applied science of *mores*, I have not held back from this problem. However, whereas in the classical school it was the starting-point, I can see it only as the end of my researches. I cannot attempt to explain the general characteristics of moral facts until I have passed carefully in review the details of moral rules (domestic, civic, professional or contractual) and have shown both the causes that give rise to them and the functions which they perform, in so far as the data of science at present permit. Thus I collect on my way a number of ideas which arise directly from the study of moral facts, and when I come to pose the general question its solution is already prepared; the solution rests on concrete realities and the mind is thus bound to see it from the correct point of view. In exposing my ideas here without having previously subjected them to these tests, I am obliged to present them rather unarmed. Where scientific demonstration is impossible I shall substitute a purely dialectical argument.

I hope, however, that among people of equal good faith dialectic is never worthless. This is particularly so in the field of morality where, despite all the facts that one may assemble, hypotheses are always so important. Finally, I have been tempted by the pedagogic side of the question. From this point of view I believe that the ideas which I shall put forward can find a place in the teaching of morality, a part of education which today lacks the degree of vitality that it needs.

[1] See p. 35.

I

Moral reality appears to us under two different aspects that must be clearly distinguished: the objective and the subjective.

Each people at a given moment of its history has a morality, and it is in the name of this ruling morality that tribunals condemn and opinion judges. For a given group there is a clearly defined morality. I postulate, then, supported by the facts, that there is a general morality common to all individuals belonging to a collectivity.

Now, apart from this morality there is an indefinite multitude of others. Each individual moral conscience expresses the collective morality in its own way. Each one sees it and understands it from a different angle. No individual can be completely in tune with the morality of his time, and one could say that there is no conscience that is not in some ways immoral. Each mind, under the influence of its milieu, education or heredity sees moral rules by a different light. One individual will feel the rules of civic morality keenly, but not so strongly the rules of domestic morality, or inversely. Another who feels only very slightly the duties of charity may have a profound respect for contract and justice. The most essential aspects of morality are seen differently by different people.

I do not intend to treat here of both these two sorts of moral reality, but only of the first. I shall deal with objective moral reality, that common and impersonal standard by which we evaluate action. The diversity of individual moral consciences shows how impossible it is to make use of them in order to arrive at an understanding of morality itself. Research into the conditions that determine these individual variations of morality would, no doubt, be an interesting psychological study, but would not help us to reach our particular goal.

Just as I am not concerned with the manner in which this or that particular individual sees morality, I also leave on one side the opinions of philosophers and moralists. I have nothing whatever to do with their systematic attempts to explain or construct moral reality except in so far as one can find in them a more or less adequate expression of the morality of their time. A moralist has a far greater sensibility than the average man to the dominant moral trends of his time, and consequently his consciousness is more representative of the moral reality. But I refuse to accept his doctrines as explanations, as scientific expressions of past or present moral reality.

The subject of my research and the kind of moral reality which I shall study have now been defined. But this reality can be studied in two different ways: (i) We can try to discover and to understand it, or (ii) we can set out to evaluate it at particular times.

Here I do not intend to discuss the second problem. We must begin with the first. Faced with the confusion of present moral ideas, a methodical approach is indispensable. We must begin at the beginning and progress from facts on which common agreement can be reached to see where the divergences occur. In order to judge or appreciate morality, as to evaluate life or nature (for value judgments can apply to the whole realm of reality), one must begin by acquainting oneself with moral reality.

Thus the first condition for the theoretical study of moral reality is to be able to recognize it and to distinguish it from other realities; in brief, to define it. This is not a question of giving it a philosophical definition; that can come when our research has made some headway. All that is possible or profitable is an initial, provisional definition that permits us to agree upon the reality we are dealing with; such a definition is obviously indispensable if we are to know what we are talking about.

The first question that confronts us, as in all rational and scientific research, is: By what characteristics can we recognize and distinguish moral facts?

Morality appears to us to be a collection of maxims, of

rules of conduct. But there are also other rules that prescribe our behaviour. All utilitarian techniques are governed
by analogous systems of rules, and we must find the
distinguishing characteristics of moral rules. If we consider
all the rules that govern conduct we shall be able to see
whether there are not some that have peculiar and specific
characteristics. If we agree that the rules that show these
characteristics conform to the popular conception[1] of moral
rules we shall be able to apply to them the usual title and to
say that here we have the characteristics of moral reality.

To achieve any result at all in this research there is only
one method of proceeding. We must discover the intrinsic
differences between these moral rules and other rules
through their apparent and exterior differences, for at the
beginning this is all that is accessible to us. We must find
a reagent that will force moral rules to demonstrate their
specific character. The reagent we shall employ is this: We
shall put these various rules to the test of violation and see
whether from this point of view there is not some difference
between moral rules and rules of technique.

The violation of a rule generally brings unpleasant consequences to the agent. But we may distinguish two different types of consequence: (i) The first results mechanically
from the act of violation. If I violate a rule of hygiene that
orders me to stay away from infection, the result of this
act will automatically be disease. The act, once it has been
performed, sets in motion the consequences, and by analysis
of the act we can know in advance what the result will be.
(ii) When, however, I violate the rule that forbids me to
kill, an analysis of my act will tell me nothing. I shall not
find inherent in it the subsequent blame or punishment.

[1] The scientific notion is not the same as the popular notion, which
may be erroneous. Popular opinion may deny the qualification *moral*
to rules which show all the signs of being moral precepts. All that is
necessary is that the difference be not so great as to render the retention of the more usual term inconvenient. Thus the zoologist may speak
of 'fish' even though his conception is not identical with the popular one.

There is complete heterogeneity between the act and its consequence. It is impossible to discover *analytically* in the act of murder the slightest notion of blame. The link between act and consequence is here a *synthetic* one.

Such consequences attached to acts by synthetic links I shall call *sanctions*. I do not as yet know the origin or explanation of this link. I merely note its existence and nature, without at the moment going any further.

We can, however, enlarge upon this notion. Since sanctions are not revealed by analysis of the act that they govern, it is apparent that I am not punished *simply because* I did this or that. It is not the intrinsic nature of my action that produces the sanction which follows, but the fact that the act violates the rule that forbids it. In fact, one and the same act, identically performed with the same material consequences, is blamed or not blamed according to whether or not there is a rule forbidding it. The existence of the rule and the relation to it of the act determine the sanction. Thus homicide, condemned in time of peace, is freed from blame in time of war. An act, intrinsically the same, which is blamed today among Europeans, was not blamed in ancient Greece since there it violated no pre-established rule.

We have now reached a deeper conception of sanctions. A sanction is the consequence of an act that does not result from the content of that act, but from the violation by that act of a pre-established rule. It is because there is a pre-established rule, and the breach is a rebellion against this rule, that a sanction is entailed.

Thus there are rules that present this particular characteristic: We refrain from performing the acts they forbid simply because they are forbidden. This is what is meant by the obligatory character of the moral rule. We rediscover by a rigorously empirical analysis the idea of *duty* and obligation almost as Kant understood it.

We have so far only considered negative sanctions (blame, punishment), since in these the characteristic of obligation is most apparent. There are sanctions of another kind. Acts that conform to the moral rule are praised and those who accomplish them are honoured. In this case the public moral consciousness reacts in a different way and the consequence of the act is favourable to the agent, but the mechanism of this social phenomenon is the same. As in the preceding instance the sanction comes, not from the act itself, but from its conformity to a rule that prescribes it. No doubt this type of obligation differs slightly from the former in degree, but we have here two varieties of the same group. There are not two kinds of moral rules, negative and positive commands; both are but two classes within the same category.

We have, then, defined moral obligation, and it is a definition not without interest. It shows how far the latest perfected utilitarian moralities have misconceived the problem of morality. Spencer's morality, for example, betrays a complete ignorance of the nature of obligation. For him punishment is no more than the mechanical consequence of an act (this is most apparent in his *Education* on the subject of school punishments[1]). This erroneous idea that punishment arises automatically from the act itself is widespread. In a recent inquiry into godless morality may be found the letter of a scientist who is interested in philosophy and maintains that the only punishment that a secular moralist can consider is the evil consequence of immoral acts (intemperance ruins the health, etc.).

In this way one evades the moral problem, which is precisely to explain duty, to explain its foundations and in what way it is not a hallucination but a reality.

So far we have followed Kant fairly closely. But if his analysis of moral acts is in part correct, it is nevertheless incomplete and insufficient, since it shows us only one aspect of moral reality.

We cannot perform an act which is not in some way

[1] *Education, Intellectual, Physical and Moral*, Ch. III, London, 1861. D.F.P.

meaningful to us simply because we have been commanded to do so. It is psychologically impossible to pursue an end to which we are indifferent—i.e. that does not appear to us as *good* and does not affect our sensibility. Morality must, then, be not only obligatory but also desirable and desired. This *desirability* is the second characteristic of all moral acts.

This desirability peculiar to moral life participates of the preceding characteristic of obligation, and is not the same as the desirability of the objects that attract our ordinary desires. The nature of our desire for the commanded act is a special one. Our *élan* and aspiration are accompanied by discipline and effort. Even when we carry out a moral act with enthusiasm we feel that we dominate and transcend ourselves, and this cannot occur without a feeling of tension and self-restraint. We feel that we do violence to a part of our being. Thus we must admit a certain element of eudemonism and one could show that desirability and pleasure permeate the obligation. We find charm in the accomplishment of a moral act prescribed by a rule that has no other justification than that it is a rule. We feel a *sui generis* pleasure in performing our duty simply because it is our duty. The notion of good enters into those of duty and obligation just as they in turn enter into the notion of good. Eudemonism and its contrary pervade moral life.

Duty, the Kantian Imperative, is only one abstract aspect of moral reality. In fact, moral reality always presents simultaneously these two aspects which cannot, in fact, be isolated. No act has ever been performed as a result of duty alone; it has always been necessary for it to appear in some respect as good. Inversely there is no act that is purely desirable, since all call for some effort.

Just as the idea of obligation, the first characteristic of moral life, gave us the opportunity to criticize utilitarianism, the second characteristic, that of goodness, shows us the insufficiency of Kant's explanation of moral obligation. Kant's hypothesis, according to which the sentiment of obligation was due to the heterogeneity of reason and sensibility, is not easy to reconcile with the fact that moral ends are in one aspect objects of desire. If to a certain extent sensibility has the same end as reason, it cannot be humbled by submitting to the latter.

Are these, then, the only two characteristics of moral reality? They are not, and I could demonstrate others. The two that I have just noted appear to me to be the most important, constant and universal. I know of no moral rule or morality where they are not found. However, in different instances they combine in varied proportions. There are acts which are accomplished almost exclusively by enthusiasm, acts of moral heroism where the element of obligation is at a minimum and where the idea of goodness predominates. There are others also where the idea of duty finds a minimum of support in the sensibility. The relation between these two elements also varies with time; thus in antiquity it would appear that the notion of duty was on the wane; in the systems of morality, and perhaps in the everyday life of the people, the idea of the Sovereign Good predominated. Generally speaking, I believe it is the same wherever morality is essentially religious. In the same epoch the relation of the two elements may vary in the extreme in different individuals. Different persons feel in different degrees the attraction of one or other of these elements, and it is very rarely indeed that both exert an equal attraction. Each one of us has his moral blind spots. There are those for whom moral acts are above all good and desirable; there are those with a greater feeling for the rule itself who enjoy discipline, loathe anything indeterminate, and wish their lives to follow a rigid programme and their conduct to be constantly controlled by inflexible rules.

This is another reason for us to be wary of the suggestions of our personal consciousness. It can easily be imagined what would be the dangers attendant upon an individual subjective method that reduced morality to the feelings that this or that person might entertain of it. There are almost always essential aspects of morality that we either do not feel at all or feel only weakly.

Having seen that these two characteristics of moral life occur wherever moral facts are found, can we say that they are on the same level? Is there one that is primary and from which the other derives? Could we, for instance, find that the idea of obligation derives from that of a desirable end? I received a letter posing this question and suggesting this hypothesis. I refuse absolutely to admit it. I will not go into all the reasons against it; since at all times, as far as we can go, we find the two characteristics co-existing, there is no objective reason for us to admit even a logical priority of one over the other. Even from the dialectical and theoretical point of view, if we have no duty except in so far as duty is desirable, the very notion of duty disappears. It is impossible to derive obligation from the desirable, since the specific characteristic of obligation is to a certain extent the violation of desire. It is as impossible to derive duty from good (or inversely) as it is to derive altruism from egoism.

It has been argued that the idea of performing an act for any other reason than its intrinsic content is incomprehensible. First of all, we are no more justified in the study of moral phenomena than in the study of psychic and other phenomena in rejecting an apparent fact simply because we are unable to give an immediate satisfactory explanation of it. To explain the characteristic of obligation in rules it is sufficient to establish the notion of moral authority. A moral authority that is legitimate in the eyes of reason receives our submission because it is moral authority and we respect its discipline. Few, I think, will deny all moral authority. That the idea of it is badly analysed is no reason for denying its existence and necessity. Later we shall see, in fact, to what observable reality this idea corresponds.

Let us then be wary of artificially simplifying moral reality. On the contrary, let us keep our attention upon the two aspects that we have noted and not become involved with their apparent contradictions. These contradictions will shortly be resolved.

Further, there is another idea that presents the same duality: the idea of the *sacred*. The sacred object inspires us, if not with fear, at least with respect that keeps us at a distance; at the same time it is an object of love and aspiration that we are drawn towards. Here, then, is a dual sentiment which seems to be self-contradictory but does not for all that cease to be real.

The human personality presents a notable example of this apparent duality which we have just distinguished. On the one hand, it inspires us with a religious respect that keeps us at some distance. Any encroachment upon the legitimate sphere of action of our fellow beings we regard as a sacrilege. It is, as it were, sacrosanct and thus apart. But at the same time human personality is the outstanding object of our sympathy and we endeavour to develop it. It is an ideal to be realized in ourselves as completely as possible.

If I compare the idea of the sacred with that of the moral, it is not merely in order to draw an interesting analogy. It is because it is very difficult to understand moral life if we do not relate it to religious life. For centuries morals and religion have been intimately linked and even completely fused. Even today one is bound to recognize this close association in the majority of minds. It is apparent that moral life has not been, and never will be, able to shed all the characteristics that it holds in common with religion. When two orders of facts have been so closely linked, when there has been between them so close a relationship for so long a time, it is impossible for them to be dissociated and become distinct. For this to happen they would have to undergo a complete transformation and so change their nature. There must, then, be morality in religion and elements of the religious in morality. In fact, present moral life abounds in the religious. These religious elements do not remain unchanged and it is certain that the religious sentiment of morality tends to become quite a different thing from that of theology. The characteristic of the sacred in morality does not lift it above criticism, as it does religion. But this is only a difference of degree and scarcely recognized by the majority even today. We may cite as proof the repugnance shown to any attempt to apply to morality the ordinary methods of science.

It would seem that in presuming to think of it and study it with the procedures of profane science we are *profaning* morality itself and threatening its dignity. Our contemporaries do not willingly admit that moral reality may, with all other realities, be submitted to discussion.

2

I have now reached the second part of my exposition, and it is here most of all that I feel certain scruples. Having determined the characteristics of moral reality, I wish to attempt some explanation of them.

The only scientific way of proceeding would be to make a list of moral rules, to classify and consider them one by one, and to try to explain the most important ones by seeking their causes and the functions they fulfil and have fulfilled. In this way we could progress to some idea of the general causes upon which depend those essential characteristics that they have in common. I have followed this method in my teaching. Being unable to follow that path here, I shall have to proceed dialectically and to admit a certain number of postulates without as rigorous a demonstration of them as I should like.

I begin with my first postulate, which is as follows: We have no duties except in relation to thinking minds; all our duties are oriented in terms of moral and thinking beings. The problem is: Who are these thinking subjects? An act can have only two ends:[1]

[1] The schema of this argument is borrowed from Wundt's *Ethik*.

   (i) The individual self.
   (ii) Beings other than myself.

Let us see first of all whether acts oriented purely in terms of myself can have a moral character. To answer this question we must examine the communal moral conscience. This method is no doubt uncertain and hazardous, since we run the risk of interpreting its answer according to our own wishes. However, honestly employed, the method is not unfruitful. First of all, probably no one will deny that no act has ever been regarded as moral which is *oriented exclusively* to the preservation of the individual. No doubt such an act becomes moral if I save myself for my family or my country, but if I save myself entirely for myself my conduct in the eyes of common opinion lacks moral value.

What then of acts directed not towards self-preservation but towards self-improvement? Again, if I try to improve myself, not from individual or even aesthetic interests but in order that this development may have a useful effect on others, then such acts will have moral value. If I try to develop my intelligence and my faculties only in order to shine and succeed my act will never be considered as moral.

Thus I, as an individual, cannot be the end of my moral conduct. Could others who, like me, are also individuals fulfil this rôle any better? If by preserving or developing my individual being as such I perform no moral act, in what way has the individuality of another any priority over mine? If of himself the agent can in no way confer a moral character on acts of which he himself is the object, why should another individual, his equal, enjoy a privilege that he himself does not possess? Between them there can be only differences of degree, which do not suffice to explain the difference in nature between *moral* and *amoral* conduct. If morality gives to the one what it refuses to the other it would rest upon a fundamental contradiction which is inadmissible not only for logical but also for practical reasons. It is difficult to see how such contradictory sentiments would not in the course of time have become aware of their contradiction. In any case it would be a singularly uncertain morality that could not be apprehended without revealing such an inconsistency.

If another individual, acting as the object of my conduct, cannot endow it with a moral character, this is no less the case when not one but several individuals are involved. If each separate individual is incapable of communicating moral value to conduct—that is to say, if he has not in himself a moral value—any number of individuals will be no more capable.

I do not maintain that opinion always refuses any moral value to acts directed towards others and towards myself. Particularly as regards the former, this would be contrary to the evidence. I do maintain that when they have a moral value they are oriented towards a higher end than the individual himself or other individuals. The morality which is recognized in them must derive from a higher source. This is apparent in acts of which I am both agent and object. If we are consistent, the same evidence applies to acts of which I am the agent but of which others are the object.

If we cannot be bound by duty except to conscious beings and we have eliminated the individual, there remains as the only other possible object of moral activity the *sui generis* collective being formed by the plurality of individuals associated to form a group. Further, the collective personality must be thought of as something other than the totality of individuals that compose it. If it were only the sum it could have no greater moral value than its component parts, which in themselves have none. We arrive then at the conclusion that if a morality, or system of obligations and duties, exists, society is a moral being qualitatively different from the individuals it comprises and from the aggregation from which it derives. The similarity between this argument and that of Kant in favour of the existence of God will be noted. Kant postulates God, since without this hypothesis morality is unintelligible. We postulate a society specifically distinct from individuals, since otherwise morality has no object and duty no roots. Let us add that this postulate is easily verified by experience. Although I have often treated this question in my books, it would be easy to give reasons other than those already advanced in defence of this conception.

This argument may be reduced to a number of very simple propositions. We return to the admission of the fact that, according to common opinion, morality begins at the same point at which disinterestedness and devotion also begin. Disinterestedness becomes meaningful only when its object has a higher moral value than we have as individuals. In the world of experience I know of only one being that possesses a richer and more complex moral reality than our own, and that is the collective being. I am mistaken; there is another being which could play the same part, and that is the Divinity. Between God and society lies the choice. I shall not examine here the reasons that may be advanced in favour of either solution, both of which are coherent. I can only add that I myself am quite indifferent to this choice, since I see in the Divinity only society transfigured and symbolically expressed.

Morality begins with life in the group, since it is only there that disinterestedness and devotion become meaningful. I speak of the life of the group generally; there are different groups—the family, the corporation, the city, the nation and the international group. A hierarchy could be established for these various groups and one would find corresponding degrees of moral activity according to the field concerned, according to the size of the society, its degree of complexity and specialization. At the moment there is little point in discussing these problems. It is enough that we mark the point where the domain of moral life appears to begin, without introducing a differentiation. Moral life begins with membership of a group, however small the group may be.

We can see now how certain acts that we have left on one side during our discussion can take on, indirectly, a moral character. The interests of others can have, we noted, no more intrinsic moral value than our own. In so far, however, as another participates in the life of the group and in so far as he is a member of the collectivity to which we are attached, he tends to take on some of its dignity and he becomes an object of our affection and interest. To be a member of the society is, as we shall shortly show, to be bound to the social ideal. There is a little of this ideal in each one of us. It is then natural that each individual participates to some extent in the religious aspect which this ideal inspires. Attachment to a group implies a necessary, if indirect, attachment to individuals. When the social ideal is a particular form of the ideal of humanity, when the type of citizen blends to a great extent with the generic type of man, it is to man as such that we find ourselves bound. This explains the moral character which is attributed to feelings of sympathy between individuals and the acts which they inspire. It is not that they themselves constitute the intrinsic elements of the moral temperament, but they are so closely—if indirectly—bound to the most essential moral attitudes that we may take their absence as very probably an index of a lesser morality. When one loves one's country or humanity one cannot see one's fellows suffer without suffering oneself and without feeling a desire to help them. But what binds us morally to others is nothing intrinsic in their empirical individuality; it is the superior end of which they are the servants and instruments.[1]

---

[1] In the same way the devotion of a scientist to his work can take on, indirectly, a moral character. The search for truth is not in itself a moral occupation; all depends upon the reason for which it is sought. It is only really and fully moral when science is revered for its beneficial effects upon society and humanity. On the other hand, the mental process involved in the self-sacrifice of the scientist impassioned by his work resembles so closely those involved in true moral self-sacrifice that it must to a certain extent participate in the feelings which the latter inspire. It is tinged with morality.

We are now in a position to understand how it is that there are rules called moral rules which we must obey because they command and which direct our actions to ends that transcend us while at the same time appearing desirable.

We have just seen that society is the end of all moral activity. Now (i) while it transcends the individual it is immanent in him; (ii) it has all the characteristics of a moral authority that imposes respect.

(i) Society transcends the individual's consciousness. It surpasses him materially because it is a result of the coalition of all the individual forces. By itself this material superiority would not be enough. The universe also surpasses the individual materially, but is not on that account called moral. Society is something more than a material power; it is a moral power. It surpasses us physically, materially and morally. Civilization is the result of the co-operation of men in association through successive generations; it is essentially a social product. Society made it, preserves it and transmits it to individuals. Civilization is the assembly of all the things to which we attach the highest price; it is the congregation of the highest human values. Because it is at once the source and the guardian of civilization, the channel by which it reaches us, society appears to be an infinitely richer and higher reality than our own. It is a reality from which everything that matters to us flows. Nevertheless it surpasses us in every way, since we can receive from this storehouse of intellectual and moral riches, of which it is the guardian, at most a few fragments only. The more we advance in time, the more complex and immense does our civilization become, and consequently the more does it transcend the individual consciousness and the smaller does the individual feel in relation to it. Each of the members of an Australian tribe carries in himself the integrated whole of his civilization, but of our present civilization each one of us can only succeed in integrating a small part.

However small it may be, we do nevertheless always

integrate in ourselves a part, and thus while society transcends us it is immanent in us and we feel it as such. While it surpasses us it is within us, since it can only exist by and through us. It is ourselves or, rather, the best part of us, since a man is only a man to the degree that he is civilized. That which makes us real human beings is the amount that we manage to assimilate of this assembly of ideas, beliefs and precepts for conduct that we call civilization. As Rousseau showed long ago: deprive man of all that society has given him and he is reduced to his sensations. He becomes a being more or less indistinct from an animal. Without language, essentially a social thing, general or abstract ideas are practically impossible, as are all the higher mental functions. Left to himself the individual would become dependent upon physical forces. If he has been able to escape, to free himself, to develop a personality, it is because he has been able to shelter under a *sui generis* force; an intense force since it results from the coalition of all the individual forces, but an intelligent and moral force capable, consequently, of neutralizing the blind and amoral forces of nature. This is the collective force. The theoretician may demonstrate that man has the right to liberty, but, whatever the value of these demonstrations, it is certain that this liberty can become a reality only in and through society.

Thus to love society is to love both something beyond us and something in ourselves. We could not wish to be free of society without wishing to finish our existence as men. I do not know whether civilization has brought us more happiness, and it is of no consequence; what is certain is that from the moment that we are civilized we can only renounce civilization by renouncing ourselves. The only question that a man can ask is not whether he can live outside society, but in what society he wishes to live. I recognize very willingly the right of the individual to live in the society of his choice, provided that he is not bound to the society of his birth by previously contracted duties.

Thus without any difficulty we have explained how society constitutes an end that surpasses us and at the same time appears to us as good and desirable, since it is bound up in the very fibres of our being. Consequently society has the essential characteristics that we have stipulated for moral ends.

(ii) But at the same time it is a moral authority; this follows from what we have already said. What is a moral authority if not the characteristic which we attribute to a real or ideal being that we conceive of as constituting a moral power superior to our own? The characteristic of all moral authority is that it imposes respect; because of this respect our will defers to its imperatives. Society, then, has all that is necessary for the transference to certain rules of conduct of that same imperative which is distinctive of moral obligation.

It remains for us now to see whether *in fact* moral rules derive from this source the authority which makes them appear to us as obligatory. As I said at first, it is impossible for me to examine this question here. All that I can say is that up to the present I have not found in my researches a single moral rule that is not the product of particular social factors. I wait for one which seems to demand another explanation to be drawn to my attention. The fact, today incontestably established, that all moral systems practised by peoples are a function of the social organization of these peoples, are bound to their social structures and vary with them, is surely proof enough. At one time, it is true, this diversity of moral systems was attributed to the ignorance or blindness of men. History has established that, except in abnormal cases, each society has in the main a morality suited to it, and that any other would not only be impossible but also fatal to the society which attempted to follow it. Individual morality, despite what is often maintained, does not escape this law, for it is social to the highest degree. What it makes us try to realize is the ideal man as the society conceives him, and each society conceives its ideal in its own image. The Roman or the Athenian ideals were closely related to the particular organizations of these two cities. This ideal type which each society demands that its members realize is the keystone of the whole social system and gives it its unity.

At the same time that we understand the two characteristics of moral facts and what these characteristics express, we also understand what constitutes their unity; they are only two aspects of one and the same reality, the collective reality. Society commands us because it is exterior and superior to us; the moral distance between it and us makes it an authority before which our will defers. But as, on the other hand, it is within us and *is* us, we love and desire it, albeit with a *sui generis* desire since, whatever we do, society can never be ours in more than a part and dominates us infinitely. Finally, from the same point of view, we can understand the sacred character which marks and has always marked moral things, the religious character without which no ethic has ever existed.

I should like to follow this up with the observation that things have no value in themselves. This is a truth which also applies in the economic sphere. The old theory of economics, according to which there were objective values inherent in things and independent of our minds, has no longer many defenders today. Values are the product of opinion; things have no value except in relation to states of mind.

At the time that manual labour was morally despised the value that was attributed to it, which expressed itself in the rate of payment, was lower than that which we nowadays recognize. One could multiply these examples.

As with economic things so with moral. When we say that they are sacred we mean that they have a value incommensurable with other human values. That which is sacred is that which is set apart, that which has nothing in common with the profane. It is evident that moral facts have this character. Never do we admit that a moral value can be expressed in terms of economic values—I would go so far as to say temporal values. We can, on occasion, excuse a man who, in the way of human weakness, neglects his duty in order to save his life; we dare never say that this sacrifice is legitimate and merits praise. This in spite of the fact that life is, of all amoral and profane goods, the one to which we cling hardest, since it is the necessary condition of the rest.

But in order that moral facts may be beyond comparison it is necessary that the sentiments that determine their value should have the same character. It is necessary that they also should be above comparison with other human desires. They must have a prestige and an energy that distinguishes them from among the other movements of our sensibility. The collective sentiments fulfil this condition. Precisely because they are the echo within us of the great voice of the collective, they speak in our consciences with a tone quite different from that of purely individual sentiments. They speak to us from a higher level and by reason of their origin they have a force and an ascendancy peculiarly their own. One can see how it is that the objects to which these sentiments attach themselves participate in the same prestige. They are set apart and elevated above other things by all the distance that separates the two different states of mind.

From this derives the characteristic sacredness with which the human being is now invested. This character is not inherent. Analyse man as he appears to empirical analysis and nothing will be found that suggests this sanctity; man is a temporal being. But under the effect of causes which it is not our business to study here the human being is becoming the pivot of social conscience among European peoples and has acquired an incomparable value. It is society that has consecrated him. Man has no innate right to this aura that surrounds and protects him against sacrilegious trespass. It is merely the way in which society thinks of him, the high esteem that it has of him at the moment, projected and objectified. Thus very far from there being the antagonism between the individual and society which is often claimed, moral individualism, the cult of the individual, is in fact the product of society itself. It is society that instituted it and made of man the god whose servant it is.

This outline may be helpful in understanding society, which for me is the source and the end of morality. I have often been accused of giving moral activity a very mediocre objective as well as a limited arena. Certainly if one sees in society only the group of individuals that compose it and their dwelling-place, the accusation is justified without difficulty. But society is different; it is above all a composition of ideas, beliefs and sentiments of all sorts which realize themselves through individuals. Foremost of these ideas is the moral ideal which is its principal *raison d'être*. To love one's society is to love this ideal, and one loves it so that one would rather see society disappear as a material entity than renounce the ideal which it embodies. Society is the field of an intense intellectual and moral life with a wide range of influence. From the actions and reactions between its individuals arises an entirely new mental life which lifts our minds into a world of which we could have not the faintest idea had we lived in isolation. This we observe best at those signal epochs of crisis when some great collective movement seizes us, lifts us above ourselves, and transfigures us. If, in the course of ordinary life, we feel its action less keenly because it is less violent and sharp, it does not for that reason cease to be real.

3

In the third part of my programme I shall be very brief. I have inserted it so that we can discuss an objection which is often made and which, I am sure, rests upon a misunderstanding.

It has been said that to see morality in this manner is to preclude all possibility of judging it. If morality is the

product of the collective, it necessarily imposes itself upon
the individual, who is in no position to question it whatever
form it may take, and must accept it passively. We are thus
condemned to follow opinion without ever having the
right to rebel against its dictates.

But here, as elsewhere, the science of reality puts us in
a position to modify the real and to direct it. The science of
moral opinion furnishes us with the means of judging it
and the need of rectifying it. I will give a few examples
of these possible rectifications.

First of all, it is possible that, as a result of some passing
upheaval, some fundamental moral principle is hidden for a
time from the public conscience which, not feeling it, denies
that it is there (theoretically and explicitly, or practically
and in action; it does not matter). The science of morals
can appeal from this temporarily troubled moral condition
to that which pre-existed in what we may call a chronic
condition. By opposing the permanence with which this
principle was held for so long with the acute and temporary
nature of the crisis during which it has been in abeyance
one can, in the name of science, awaken rational doubts
as to the legitimacy of its negation. One can always by the
same method do more, and show how this principle is
related to such or such essential and ever-present conditions
of our social organization and collective mentality; how,
in fact, one cannot ignore it without at the same time misunderstanding the conditions by which the collective, and
hence the individual, exists. Let us suppose that at a given
time the society as a whole tends to lose sight of the sacro-
sanctity of individual rights. Could we not correct it with
authority by reminding it that the rights of the individual
are so closely bound to the structure of the great European
societies and our whole mentality that to deny them, under
the pretext of social interests, is to deny the most essential
interests of society itself?

It is equally possible that, apart from the present existing
order of morality maintained by the forces of tradition,

new tendencies more or less conscious of themselves are appearing. The science of morals allows us to take up a position between these two divergent moralities, the one now existing and the one in the process of becoming. It teaches us, for example, that the first is related to an order which has disappeared or is disappearing, and that the new ideas on the contrary are related to recent changes in the conditions of collective existence and are made necessary by these changes. Our science may help us to render these ideas more precise and to direct them, etc.

We are not then obliged to bend our heads under the force of moral opinion. We can even in certain cases feel ourselves justified in rebelling against it. It may, in fact, happen that, for one of the reasons just indicated, we shall feel it our duty to combat moral ideas that we know to be out of date and nothing more than survivals. The best way of doing this may appear to be the denial of these ideas, not only theoretically but also in action. No doubt here I am touching on points of conscience that are always delicate, and I do not intend to resolve the problem in a word. I wish merely to indicate that the method I have laid down permits the posing of these problems.

But in any case we cannot aspire to a morality other than that which is related to the state of our society. We have here an objective standard with which to compare our evaluations. The reason which is the judge on these matters is not the individual reason, subject as it is to all sorts of private aspirations and personal preferences, but the reason supported by the methodical observation of a given reality, the social reality. It is from society and not from the individual that morality derives. No doubt we shall often be bound to take sides on these questions without waiting for our science to be sufficiently advanced to guide us; the necessity for action often forces us to precede science. In such cases we do what we can; we replace methodical science, in the circumstances impossible, by a more summary and premature science which looks in moments of doubt to the inspirations of sensibility. I am not trying to suggest that this new-born science is already in a condition to act as the sovereign guide of conduct. All I want to show here is that this science, far from preventing us from evaluating reality, gives us the means by which we can arrive at *reasoned* evaluations.

Such then—as far as it can be outlined in the course of a lecture—is the general conception of moral facts to which research on this subject for a little over twenty years has led me. It has been judged as narrow; I hope that better understanding will not see it as such. We have seen, on the contrary, that without making itself systematically eclectic it finds room for points of view which ordinarily appear completely opposed. I wish to stress the fact that this science permits the empirical study of moral facts, while at the same time not destroying the *sui generis* religious character which is inherent in them and which distinguishes them from all other human phenomena. Thus we escape from utilitarian empiricism which, while claiming to offer a rational explanation of morality, denies its specific characteristics and reduces its fundamental ideas to those of economic techniques, as also from Kantian *a priorism*, which gives a fairly faithful analysis of the nature of morality but which describes more than it explains. We recognize the notion of duty, but for experimental reasons and without rejecting the valuable aspect of eudemonism. The fact of the matter is this: the different points of view which among moralists are in opposition are mutually exclusive only in the abstract. In fact they only express different aspects of a complex reality, and consequently all will be found in their various places when one brings one's mind to bear on this reality which one wishes to understand in its complexity.

III

REPLIES TO OBJECTIONS[1]

1. The Condition of Society and the Condition of Social Opinion

I HAVE said that the point of departure for our predictions regarding the future of morality should be not social opinion but the state of the society, either as it actually exists or as it can be said to be becoming by virtue of the inevitable causes that govern its evolution. What we have to discover is society as it is, not society as it sees itself, which may produce an erroneous picture. For example, the problem nowadays is to discover what should be the fate of morality in a society like our own, characterized by a growing concentration and unification, by the increase of possibilities of communication which bring into relation the different parts and further the absorption of local life in the general, by the rise of powerful industries, and the development of individualism which accompanies this centralization of all the social forces, etc.

The confused social aspirations which make themselves heard on all sides express the way in which society, or rather its different parts, sees the actual condition and the way in which it is to be faced. They have no other value. Certainly they are valuable sources of information in that they convey some part of the underlying social reality, but

[1] Part of the Discussion on 27 March, 1906, which followed Durkheim's address to the *Société Française de Philosophie* on 11 February. We have retained only the longer of Durkheim's replies and those which seem to throw more light on his theory of a science of morality. The sub-titles are ours. The first extract is in answer to an observation by M. Parodi.

each only expresses one aspect and not always very faith-fully. Everyday passions and prejudices do not allow of an exact expression. To science alone belongs the task of discovering the reality itself and of expressing it. It is on the reality, thus understood, that the scientist should base his judgments of future developments. I do not deny that, in order to study the practical moral problem of today, it is as well to understand the various manifestations of Socialism as well as those of its opponents, and also current religious thought, etc. But the scientist may be sure, in advance, that not one of these different causes will, in its spontaneous form, satisfy him. One of them may show more practical truth than the others and for that reason merit a certain amount of preference.

The role of science does not stop at throwing a little more light upon the tendencies of public opinion, for the primary object of its investigations is the condition of the society and not that of social opinion. It would be difficult to argue that social opinion contains no part of the reality and that the aspirations of the collective conscience are mere hallucinations. Although they do not determine scientific research it is to be foreseen that the results of this research, if it is methodical, will come up against certain of them and that then it will be necessary to clarify and complete the one by the other. Furthermore, if the scientist or the philosopher has advocated a morality which has no relation to opinion, the work will be in vain, since the morality in question will remain a dead letter. Such a discordance should suffice to put a prudent and methodical mind on its guard against its own conclusions, however clearly deduced they may appear to be. Thus it is that, *in practice*, the role of reason has always been more or less to help the age to be more aware of itself, its needs and its sentiments. The science of morality, as I understand it, is the more methodical application of reason to this same end.

Socrates expressed, more clearly than his judges, the

morality suited to his time. It would be easy to show that, as a result of the transformation of the old society based on the *gens* and the consequent disturbance of religious beliefs, a new morality and religious faith had become necessary in Athens. It would be equally simple to demonstrate that this aspiration towards a new formulation was not felt by Socrates alone, but that there was already a powerful current represented by the attitudes of the Sophists. It is in this sense that Socrates was ahead of his time while at the same time expressing its spirit.

2. INDIVIDUAL REASON AND MORAL REALITY[1]

The individual can free himself partially from the rules of society if he feels the disparity between them and society as it is, and not as it appears to be—that is, if he desires a morality which corresponds to the actual state of the society and not to an outmoded condition. The principle of rebellion is the same as that of conformity. It is the *true* nature of society that is conformed to when the traditional morality is obeyed, and yet it is also the *true* nature of society which is being conformed to when the same morality is flouted. . . .

In the sphere of morality, as in the other spheres of nature, *individual* reason has no particular prestige as such. The only reason for which one can claim the right of intervention, and of rising above historical moral reality in order to reform it, is not my reason nor yours; it is the impersonal human reason, only truly realized in science. In the same way that the natural sciences permit us to manipulate the material with which they deal, so the science of moral facts puts us in a position to order and direct the course of moral life. The intervention of science has as its end, not the substitution of an individual ideal for the collective, but the substitution of an equally collective ideal which expresses not a particular personality but the collective itself more clearly understood.

[1] Reply to an observation made by M. Darlu.

The science of moral facts,[1] as I understand it, is simply this: the application of human reason to the moral order, first of all to understand it, and finally to direct its changes. I am not concerned with 'the literal meaning of reason'. On the contrary, this methodical application of the reason has, as its principal task, our release from the suggestions of 'reason' thus understood, in order to allow the things themselves to speak; the things in this case being the present condition of moral opinion in its relation to the social reality which it should express. . . .

There is between us a difference which it would be better to bring to the surface rather than to hide. A rebellion against the traditional morality you conceive of as a revolt of the individual against the collective, of personal sentiments against collective sentiments. However, what I am opposing to the collective is the collective itself, but more and better aware of itself. If it is argued that this fuller and higher consciousness of itself is only expressed in and through an individual intellect, I reply that society arrives at this fuller consciousness only by science; and science is not an individual; it is a social thing, pre-eminently impersonal.

Certainly the role which I ascribe to reason is a considerable one. First, however, I must explain what I mean by reason. If what is meant by the word is a moral faculty which contains, in an immanent state, a moral ideal, the *true* ideal which it is able to oppose, and should oppose, to that which society follows at each moment of its history, I say that this *a priorism* is an arbitrary affirmation which all known facts contradict. The reason to which I make

---

[1] The precise meaning of the following paragraph is obscure. We have not the text of M. Darlu's objection which would clarify it. Durkheim, apparently quoting from it, refers to *sens propre* and we suppose has suggested a distinction between his own understanding of the word 'reason' and that of Darlu. It is possible Darlu suggested that reason, literally understood, is a moral faculty. This supposition is strengthened by the argument of the next paragraph but one. The distinction in French is between *sens propre* and *sens figuré*, the literal and the figurative meaning.—D. F. P.

my appeal is reason applying itself to a given matter in a methodical manner in order to understand the nature of past and present morality, and which draws from this theoretical study its practical consequences. Reason thus understood is simply science, the science of morality. My major concern is to free morality from sentimental subjectivism, which hinders its progress and is a form either of empiricism or mysticism, two closely linked ways of thinking.

Moreover, in expressing myself thus, I do not say that we must leave the reformation of morality until our science is sufficiently advanced for us to propose useful reforms. We must live, and we must often anticipate science. In such cases we must do as we can and make use of what scientific observations are at our disposal, completing them by our impressions and sensations, etc. It is true that we run a risk, but that is inevitable. All that I wish to prove is that the attitude which I adopt in the study of moral facts does not condemn me to a sort of resigned optimism. . . .

M. Darlu proposes as evidence that there is more in the mind 'of an individual than in the most perfect and complex society'. I must confess that to me it is the exact opposite which has always appeared to be obvious. The assembly of moral and intellectual benefits which constitute civilization at each moment of its history has its seat in the collective mind, not in the individual. Each one of us succeeds only in assimilating a fragment of the knowledge, is only susceptible to certain aesthetic impressions. It is in the society, and through the society, that knowledge and art exist in their fullness. People talk of the moral richness of the individual! But of the many moral currents that traverse our epoch each of us realizes only the one which happens to cross his individual milieu, and has only a fragmentary and superficial notion of that. How much richer and more complex is the moral life of society, with all its different complementary or conflicting moral currents! But we know practically nothing of this intense activity which ferments about us. . . .

Of all moral rules those which concern the individual ideal most clearly demonstrate their social origin. The man that we try to be is the man of our times and of our milieu. No doubt each of us in his different way colours this communal ideal with his own individuality, in the same way that each of us practises charity, justice, patriotism, etc., in his own way. However, so far from the ideal being an individual construction, it is that in which the different members of the group communicate; it is that which above all gives them their moral unity. The Roman had his ideal of perfection which was related to the constitution of the Roman city, just as ours is related to the structure of contemporary society. It is a gross illusion to believe that we have freely conceived it in our conscience.

3. THE FEELING OF OBLIGATION: THE SACRED CHARACTER OF MORALITY [1]

The feeling of obligation varies without ceasing, and often, if one loses sight of this characteristic variability, one imagines that it has ceased to exist simply because it is modified. This is what is happening today in French society. I am very much struck by the fact that it is the other aspect of morality, the desirable, that preponderates among our contemporaries. This is a condition for which it would not be impossible to give reasons.

For the feeling of obligation to appear in all its strength there must exist a closely wrought moral system prevailing without opposition. Today traditional morality is shaken and no other has been brought forward to replace it. The old duties have lost their power without our being able to see clearly and with assurance where our new duties lie. Different minds hold opposed ideas and we are passing through a period of crisis. It is not then surprising that we

[1] In reply to an observation made by M. Jacob.

do not feel the pressure of moral rules as they were felt in the past. They cannot appear to us in their old majesty, since they are practically non-existent. From this it results that morality appears to us less as a code of duties, a defined discipline, than as an attracting ideal, half glimpsed at. The incentive to a moral life is not so much a feeling of deference to an uncontested imperative, but rather a sort of aspiration towards an elevated but vague objective. Let us, however, remind ourselves of the dangers attendant upon drawing conclusions from such a limited and superficial experience.

Having made these observations, I come to the heart of the question that M. Jacob has asked me.

Certainly I will maintain the sacred character of morality. I base my opinion, not upon any feeling that I personally may have, but upon the facts. It is impossible to imagine, on the evidence, that morality should entirely sever its unbroken historic association with religion without ceasing to be itself. A fact cannot lose one of its essential attributes without changing its nature. Morality would no longer be morality if it had no element of religion. Apart from this, the horror which crime inspires is in all ways comparable to that with which a believer reacts to sacrilege. The respect which we have for the human being is distinguishable only very slightly from that which the faithful of all religions have for the objects they deem sacred. This characteristic, sacredness, can be expressed, I believe—and I feel bound to express it—in secular terms. That is, in fact, the distinctive mark of my attitude. Instead of joining with the utilitarians in misunderstanding and denying the religious element in morality, or hypostatizing with theology a transcendent Being, I feel it necessary to translate it in rational language without thereby destroying any of its peculiar characteristics. You will see that, from this point of view, I escape the objection you have made since, confronted with the sacred, of which I affirm the existence, my secular reason retains all its independence.

8

Is this enterprise possible? Is it not, as you seem to believe, contradictory in its terms?

In order to reply to this question I shall have to give a rather closer definition of the sacred. I do not, of course, hope to give here a rigorous definition. It is, however, possible to establish certain characteristics which will help me to explain myself.

First of all, I would like to point out that you seem to identify the idea of the sacred with that of obligation, with the categorical imperative. Such an identification would call for an explanation. You would have to show, for instance, that the imperative was, in fact, the religious element in morality. However, one could demonstrate that the more sacred a moral rule becomes, the more the element of obligation tends to recede. Very often the sanction that applies to the violation of ritual precepts is analogous to that attached to the violation of the rules of hygiene. The unwise man who exposes himself to infection contracts the disease as the direct result of his contact with it. In the same way the layman who profanely touches some sacred object releases against himself a terrible force that deals upon him disease and death. The prophylactics of religion and of medicine are similar in many ways. It is not then because of its characteristic of obligation that morality is related to religion.

The sacred, as I have said elsewhere in this discussion, is that which is *set apart*, that which is *separated*. What characterizes it is that it cannot, without losing its nature, be mixed with the profane. Any mixture, or even contact, *profanes* it, that is to say, destroys its essential attributes. But this separation does not leave the two orders of being that have been separated upon the same level. We see this from the solution of continuity that exists between the sacred and the profane. There is between them no common measure, they are heterogeneous and incommensurable; the value of the sacred cannot be compared with that of the profane.

This being so, how is it that there are no incommensurable secular values? If there are any, they are sacred. It is in this way that an element of the religious can enter into morality.

That moral phenomena correspond to this definition, that they are incommensurable with other natural phenomena, seems to be incontestable. It is a fact. The public conscience does not admit, and has never admitted, that one would be justified in failing in one's duty for purely utilitarian reasons. If it is forced to tolerate such behaviour, it seeks, by means of some casuistry, to hide the contradiction from itself. Thus sacredness and morality are closely related. But reason has never abdicated its rights before this sacredness. The reason why we attach this character to certain objects or to certain acts; how it is that there exists this separate world of *sui generis* representations; and to what in the world of reality these representations correspond, is a legitimate study. It is precisely this question that I have tried to answer. We might even go further and wonder whether certain things and ways of acting, which today possess this character, possess it unjustly as survivals or as a result of abnormal circumstances; whether certain others which do not possess it at the moment do not look as though they are destined to acquire it, etc. Reason, then, maintains all its liberty even while it sees in moral reality a sacred quality which effects a solution of continuity between morality and economic and industrial techniques, etc., which current utilitarianism tends to confuse.

The science of which I speak is not general sociology, and I am not trying to say that research into social structures and political and economic systems will produce deductions as to the moral system. The only science that will furnish methods of approaching these judgments on moral matters is the special science of moral facts. In order to understand morality we must proceed from the moral data of the present and the past. Certainly this science of moral facts is, I am convinced, a sociological science, but it is a very particular branch of sociology. The *sui generis* character which I see in moral phenomena does not allow us to make deductions regarding it from other phenomena. Moral facts are related to other social facts, and it is not a question of abstracting them, but they form, in the society, a distinct sphere. Practical speculations relating to this sphere can only be inferred from theoretical speculations equally related to the same order of facts.

M. Brunschwig having proposed to define the progress of civilization as consisting in its ability to permit 'to individual freedom (libertés individuelles) *more and more the exercise of its right of resumption against the material structure of society', M. Durkheim replied:*

This expression *resumption* seems to me to be very inexact. It is not a matter of resumption but of an accession made by the grace of society. These rights and liberties are not things inherent in man as such. If you analyse man's constitution you will find no trace of this sacredness with which he is invested and which confers upon him these rights. This character has been added to him by society. Society has consecrated the individual and made him pre-eminently worthy of respect. His progressive emancipation does not imply a weakening but a transformation of the social bonds. The individual does not tear himself from society but is joined to it in a new manner, and this is because society sees him in a new manner and wishes this change to take place.

The individual submits to society and this submission is the condition of his liberation. For man freedom consists in deliverance from blind, unthinking physical forces; this he achieves by opposing against them the great and intelligent force which is society, under whose protection he shelters. By putting himself under the wing of society, he makes himself also, to a certain extent, dependent upon it. But this is a liberating dependence. There is no paradox here.

4. THE MORAL AUTHORITY OF THE COLLECTIVE [1]

I did not say that the moral authority of society derives from its role as moral legislator; that would be absurd. I said, on the contrary, that society is qualified to play the part of legislator because in our eyes it is invested with a well-founded moral authority. The term 'moral authority' is opposed to material authority or physical supremacy. Moral authority is a psychic reality, a higher and richer conscience than our own, one upon which we feel that our own depends. I have shown how society presents this characteristic because it is the source and seat of all the intellectual benefits that constitute civilization. From society derive all the essentials of our mental life. Our individual reason is, and has the same value as, that collective and impersonal reason called science which is, both in its constitution and in its processes, pre-eminently a social thing. Our aesthetic faculties, the fineness of our taste, derive from art, which is again a social thing. It is to society that we owe the power over matter which is our glory. It is society that has freed us from nature. Is it not then to be expected that we think of it as a mental being higher than ourselves from which our mental powers emanate? This explains why it is that when it demands of us those sacrifices, great or small, that make up our moral life, we bow before its demands with deference.

The believer bows before his God, because it is from God that he believes that he holds his being, particularly his mental being, his soul. We have the same reasons for experiencing this feeling before the collective.

I do not know what an ideal and absolute perfection is, and therefore I do not ask you to conceive of society as ideally perfect. I do not even attribute to it, any more than to ourselves, relative perfection; all this is beside the ques-

[1] In reply to an observation made by M. Malapert.

tion. Society has its pettiness and it has its grandeur. In order for us to love and respect it, it is not necessary to present it other than it is. If we were only able to love and respect that which is *ideally perfect*, supposing the word to have any definite meaning, God Himself could not be the object of such a feeling, since the world derives from Him and the world is full of imperfection and ugliness.

It is true that it is a common practice to speak of society with disdain. Then it is seen only as a bourgeois administration with the gendarme to protect it. This is to neglect, without even seeing it, the most rich and complex moral reality that we have ever had a chance of observing.

It is unquestionable that, as regards our present moral conscience, morality itself, entire and as complete as we can conceive it, presupposes that from the moment we conform to a moral rule we not only desire to conform to it but also desire the rule itself. This would not be possible if we did not understand the reasons that justify the rule and judge them to be well founded. It is as well to recognize, however, that this implies an ideal understanding which, whatever our conception of morality may be, we are at present very far from attaining. We do not know—and this is a confession of ignorance which would be preferable in our schools to the over-simplified and often puerile explanations with which we too often deceive the curiosity of youth—we know nothing whatsoever either of the historical causes or of the teleological reasons that in fact justify the greater part of our moral institutions. Once one has left abstract discussion where theories of morality too often stop short, one cannot but feel that it is impossible to understand the *why* of the family, marriage, the laws of property, etc., either in their present forms or in the new functions that they are called upon to fulfil, without taking into account the social environment which is only now beginning to be studied. In this all the various schools are in the same predicament. There is, then, a *desideratum* of

the moral conscience that I am far from under-estimating;
it is one that we are all not in a position to satisfy at the
present time in a satisfactory manner. The method which
I employ does not put me at all in a weak position on this
point so long as one does not consider it an advantage to
close one's eyes to difficulty. Further, I believe that it is
the only method that will allow of a progressive resolution
of the problem.

5. PHILOSOPHY AND MORAL FACTS [1]

You are in fact asking me a double question: first, why
I dismiss the theories of philosophers, and secondly,
where I intend to find the moral facts that I intend to
study. I shall deal with the first question first.

The comparison which you make between the moral
philosopher on the one side and the physician or astronomer on the other, the comparison upon which your
argument rests, seems to me to be quite erroneous. No
doubt if I wished to acquaint myself with the facts of
astronomy, I should go to an astronomer and not to a
fellow ignoramus. But the only reason for the existence of
the science of astronomy is to express, objectively and
adequately, astronomic reality. The objective pursued at
all times by moral philosophers is quite different in
nature. They have never set up as their goal the faithful
representation, without addition or subtraction, of a given
moral reality. The ambition of moral philosophers has
more often been to construct a new morality, a morality
differing in essential points from that followed by their
contemporaries or by their predecessors. They have rather
been revolutionaries or iconoclasts. The problem that I
am concerned with is that of discovering in what morality
consists or has consisted. Not, that is, as it has been
conceived by some individual philosopher, but as it has

[1] In reply to an observation made by M. Weber.

been lived by humanity in the collective. From this point of view the doctrines of philosophers lose a great deal of their value. If the science of *morals and law*, as we are trying to make it, were sufficiently advanced, it would be able to play in relation to moral facts the same role that astronomy plays in relation to astronomical facts. One would go to it in order to discover in what moral life consists. But this science of morality is only now being born, and the theories of philosophers coincide so little with our intentions, so little do they set themselves the object that we have in view, that they are unanimously opposed to our way of looking at and studying moral facts. They cannot, then, serve us as authorities in the same way.

However, it would be very wrong to suppose that I exclude them completely. I only deny them the prerogative and primacy that has too often been accorded to them. They also are instructive as facts. They teach us what passes in the public mind of one particular epoch and they must therefore be accounted for. What I refuse to admit is that they express moral truth in a particularly eminent manner, in the same way that physics or chemistry expresses the truth about the order of things coming under the head of the physico-chemical.

The opposition which you make of the religious fact to the moral seems to me to be inadmissible. There is no rite, however material it be, that does not form a part of a more or less organized system of representations that will explain and justify it. Man needs to understand what he does, though often he is easily satisfied; this is often the reason lying behind a myth. If you admit that a religious fact can be approached apart from the theories that attempt to explain it, why should it be otherwise with moral facts?

However, I do not suppose that you would dream of denying the existence of a moral reality beyond the minds of the philosophers who try to express it. We all practise this morality without troubling, for the most part, about the reasons given by philosophers to justify it. The proof of this is the embarrassment we should feel if anyone were to demand of us a solid rational justification of the moral rules that we observe.

There remains the question of the methods which will enable us to arrive at this moral reality. It is certainly a delicate, but not insoluble, question. There is first of all a considerable number of ideas and moral maxims that are easily accessible, those that are written down and those that are condensed in legal formulas. In law the greater part of domestic morality, the morality of contract and obligation, all the ideas relating to the great fundamental duties, are translated and reflected. Already there is ample material for our consideration which will satisfy a great part of our scientific ambitions for some time. When we have broken this new ground we will pass on to another. I do not deny that there are duties and moral ideas that are not formulated in law, but these must be reached by other methods. Proverbs, popular maxims and non-codified customs are no less sources of information. Literary works, the conceptions of philosophers and moralists (you observe that I do not exclude them), direct our attention to aspirations that are only at the stage of attempting self-realization. They help us to go further in our analysis of the communal conscience to that substratum where these obscure and only half-conscious currents are elaborated. It may seem that these are clumsy methods that stand little chance of discovering all the subtleties and shades of moral reality, but this is a difficulty that faces all science at the outset. We have first of all to cut broad avenues that may bring in some light to this virgin forest of moral and, more generally, social facts.

6. THE SUBJECTIVE REPRESENTATION
OF MORALITY [1]

At the outset I said that we have to distinguish two equally true aspects of morality:

(i) Objective morality consisting of a number of rules and forming the morality of the group;

(ii) The subjective manner in which each individual conscience conceives this morality.

In fact, while there is a morality of the group, held in common by all its members, each individual has, to a certain extent, his own morality. Even where conformity is highest, each individual constructs, in part, his own morality. Each one of us has his own inner moral life and there is no individual conscience that exactly translates the communal moral conscience, which is not, that is to say, in some degree inadequate. From this point of view, as I have already indicated, each one of us is immoral in certain respects. I am, then, far from denying the existence of this interior moral life; I do not deny that one could study it with success, but this field of study is beyond our researches and I leave it on one side, at least for the moment.

It is this field, however, which M. Rauh has touched upon, and from the observation of several individual moral consciences he has arrived at a conclusion that seems to me to be very questionable. He argues that, from observing the behaviour of certain individuals (scholars, artists), he has ascertained that they consider some of the duties that they perform to be absolutely extra-social ones. From this M. Rauh concludes that there really are some duties which exist independently of the collective life and which are born as a direct result of man's relations with the world. First of all, I do not know why M. Rauh has limited his examples to the special milieu of scholars and artists. As a matter

[1] In reply to an observation made by M. Rauh.

of fact this way of looking at things is very general. There is only a very small number of individuals who feel that their duties have a social origin. The majority see it quite differently, and it is from this difference that all the opposition to my idea has arisen.

It remains only to see whether their picture of morality is an illusion. M. Rauh has undertaken to demonstrate that a sociological explanation of these duties is impossible. I will not discuss his demonstration in detail because it seems to me to go against the well-known principle that there is no negative experience. I understand that one can prove to be erroneous an explanation that has been offered, but I find it difficult to conceive how one can *a priori* oppose an explanation not yet offered and presuppose that, whatever form it may take, it is impossible.

IV

VALUE JUDGMENTS
AND JUDGMENTS OF REALITY [1]

IN submitting to the Congress this subject for discussion I am setting myself a double goal: first, to show by specific example how sociology can help to resolve a problem of philosophy, and, secondly, to remove certain prejudices under which so-called positive sociology too often suffers.

When we say that bodies are heavy, that the volume of gas varies in inverse proportion to the pressure applied to it, we make judgments which are limited to the expression of facts. They are judgments which define what is, and for this reason they are called judgments of existence or of reality.

Other judgments do not have for object the nature of things, but rather their worth in relation to persons—i.e. the value which the latter attach—and these are called value judgments. This name is often extended to any judgment which reports an estimation, whatever it may be. This extension of the term makes for confusions against which we must be on our guard.

When I say, 'I like hunting', 'I prefer beer to wine', 'an active life to one of repose' etc., I express judgments which might appear to be based upon estimations but which are, in fact, simple judgments of reality. They merely report my relations with certain objects: that I like this or prefer that. These preferences are facts as much as the heaviness of bodies or the elasticity of gas. Such judgments do not

[1] A lecture given to the International Congress of Philosophy at a general meeting at Bologna on 6 April and published in a special number of the *Revue de Métaphysique et de Morale*, 3 July, 1911.

attach value to objects but merely affirm the state of the subject. Also the predilections which are expressed are not communicable. Those who experience them can say that they experience them or, at least, that they think they do; but they cannot communicate their experience to others. It is part of their personality and cannot be divorced from it.

It is quite a different matter when I say: 'This man *has* a high moral value, this picture *has* great aesthetic value, this jewel is *worth* so much.' In all these instances I attribute to the people or things in question an objective character quite independent of my own individual feelings at the time of making the judgment. I personally may not attach any value to a jewel; but its value is not the less for that. I as an individual may not be highly moral in my behaviour, but that does not prevent me from recognizing moral value when I see it. By temperament I may not be very sensitive to art, but that is no reason why I should deny that there can be aesthetic value. All these values exist then, in a sense, outside me. Thus when we are in disagreement with others over judgments in such matters we try to communicate our convictions. We are not satisfied with merely affirming their existence; we try to demonstrate their validity by supporting them with impersonal arguments. Implicitly we recognize that these judgments correspond to some objective reality upon which agreement can and should be reached. These *sui generis* realities constitute values, and it is to these realities that value judgments refer.

We must see how it is that such judgments are possible, and the terms of the problem are implicit in what has gone before. On the one hand, all value presupposes appreciation by an individual in relation with a particular sensibility. What has value is in some way good; what is good is desired, and all desire is a psychological state. Nevertheless the values under discussion have the objectivity of things. How can these two characteristics, which at first blush appear contradictory, be reconciled? How, in fact, can a state of feeling be independent of the subject that feels it?

To this problem two contradictory solutions have been given.

I

For many thinkers of heterogeneous schools of thought the difference between these two types of judgment is only apparent. Value, it is said, is inherent in some constituent characteristic of the object to which value is attributed, and a value judgment expresses no more than the effect of this characteristic upon the subject that judges. If this effect is favourable a positive value is ascribed, if unfavourable, a negative value. If life has value for a man, it is because man is a living creature and it is in the nature of the living to live. If corn has value it is because it is food and maintains life. If justice is a virtue, it is because justice respects the vital interests; for the opposite reason homicide is a crime. The value of a thing would, in fact, appear to be simply the realization of the effects that it produces as a result of its intrinsic properties.

But what is the *subject* in relation to which the value of these things is, and should be, estimated?

If it is to be the individual, how can we explain the existence of a system of objective values, recognized by all men, or at least by all the men of the same civilization? For, from this point of view, value consists in the effect of the thing upon the sensibility, but the great diversity of individual sensibilities is well known. What pleases some revolts others. Life itself is not desired by all, for there are those who, either out of disgust or duty, throw it away. Above all, there is great variety in the manner of its appreciation. One may like it intense and complex, another's pleasure lies in simplicity. This objection to the utilitarian ethic has been made too often for us to be occupied with it here. We will point out only that it is an objection that applies with equal force to any theory that claims to explain, by purely psychological causes, economic, aesthetic or philosophical values. It might be argued that there is a *mean type* found in the majority of individuals, and that the objective evaluation of things expresses the effect that they have upon the average individual. There is, however, an enormous gap between the way in which values are, in fact, estimated by the ordinary individual and the objective scale of human values which should in principle govern our judgments. The average moral conscience is mediocre; it feels only slightly the commonest duties and hence the corresponding moral values; it is as though it were blind to some of them. We cannot therefore look to the average for a standard of morality. This applies with greater conviction to the aesthetic values that are, for the majority, a dead letter. For economic values the distance, in certain cases, is perhaps less considerable. However, it is obvious that it is not the physical properties of the diamond or the pearl, acting upon the majority of our contemporaries, that explains the present value of these things.

There is, however, another reason why objective evaluation and average evaluation should not be confused: it is that the reactions of the average individual continue to be individual reactions. Because a certain condition is found in a large number of people, it is not for that reason objective. Simply because there are many people who like something in a certain way, it does not follow that that appreciation has been imposed upon them by some external reality. This phenomenon of unanimity may be entirely due to subjective causes, notably a sufficient homogeneity of individual temperaments. Between 'I like this' and 'a certain number of us like this' there is no essential difference.

It has been believed possible to escape these difficulties by substituting the society for the individual. As in the preceding theory, it is maintained that value is intrinsic in some element of the thing judged. In this case it is from the way in which the thing affects the collective subject, and no longer the individual, that the value is derived. The estimate becomes objective by being a collective one.

This theory has certain incontestable advantages over the preceding one. Social judgment is objective as compared with individual judgment. The scale of values is thus released from the variable and subjective evaluations of individuals. The latter find outside themselves an established classification which is not their own work, which expresses other than their own personal sentiments, and to which they are bound to conform. The opinion of society derives from its origins a moral authority by virtue of which it imposes itself upon the individual. It resists attempts to disturb it, and reacts against dissentients just as all the world resents the non-conformer. It blames those whose evaluation of moral facts is based on principles other than those it prescribes, and ridicules those whose aesthetic inspiration is different. Whoever tries to obtain something at less than its worth runs up against a resistance similar to that of a material object. Thus may be explained that awareness of external constraint operating when we make a value judgment. We know very well that we are not the masters of our evaluations, that we are bound and constrained. It is the social conscience that binds us.

This aspect of the value judgment is not the only one, for there is another almost opposed to the first. These same values which, on the one hand, have the effect of realities imposed upon us, on the other hand appear to us as things which we like and naturally desire. The fact is that society is at the same time a legislator to whom we owe respect and also the creator and guardian of all those goods of civilization to which we are bound with all the strength of our souls. Society is a benefactor as well as a master. Whatever increases the vitality of the society increases our vitality. It is not therefore surprising that the society and its members should attach value to the same things.

But, thus understood, a sociological theory of values raises in its turn certain grave difficulties. These are, moreover, not peculiar to it in that the same objections may be directed against the preceding psychological theory.

There are different types of value. Economic, moral, religious, aesthetic and speculative values are all different. The attempts to reduce the one to the other, ideas of goodness, beauty, truth and utility, have always proved abortive. If what determines value is only the way in which things affect the working of the social life, the diversity of values becomes hard to explain. If the same cause is at work in every case, whence arise effects so specifically different?

Again, if the value of a thing is determined by the degree of its social (or individual) utility, the system of human values would be shaken and changed from top to bottom. The place given to luxury would from this point of view become unjustified and incomprehensible. By definition what is superfluous is not useful or is less useful than what is necessary. Surplus in any form may be lacking without the vital functions being seriously disturbed. In a word, luxuries are by nature costly and cost more than they return. We find doctrinaire spirits who despise them and who try to reduce them to a more congruous position, but in fact there is nothing that has more value in the eyes of man. All art is a luxury; aesthetic activity is not subordinated to any useful end; it is released for the sole pleasure of the release. What is pure speculation if not thought exercising itself quite free from any utilitarian goal? Yet who can deny that humanity has always esteemed artistic and speculative values much more highly than economic? Like the intellect, the moral sphere has an aesthetic peculiar to itself. The highest virtue consists not in the strict and regular performance of those acts immediately necessary to the well-being of the social order, but rather in those free and spontaneous movements and sacrifices which are not demanded and are sometimes even

9

contrary to the principles of a sound economy. There is virtue that is folly, and it is in its folly that its grandeur consists. Spencer has shown that philanthropy is often not in the best interests of society. His demonstration will not prevent men from esteeming the virtue he condemns very highly. Economic life itself does not always follow closely the rules of economics. If luxuries are those things that cost most, it is not only because they are often the most rare; it is because they are also the most esteemed. Life as man at all times has conceived it is not simply a precise arrangement of the budget of the individual or social organism, the reaction with the least possible expense to the outside stimulus, the careful balance between debit and credit. To live is above all things to act, to act without counting the cost and for the pleasure of acting. If the evidence demands that we do not discount economy, as man must amass in order to expend, nevertheless that expenditure is his end, and to expend is to act.

Let us go further and examine all these theories for the fundamental principle underlying them. We find that all equally presuppose that the value of a thing is inherent in, and expresses the nature of, that thing. This postulate is, however, contrary to the facts. There are many instances in which no such relation exists between the characteristics of an object and the value attributed to it.

An idol is a very sacred object and sacredness the highest value ever recognized by man. An idol is often, however, nothing but a block of stone or a piece of wood, things which in themselves have no value. There is no order of being, however humble or commonplace, that has not at some time in our history inspired sentiments of religious respect. The most useless or harmless animals, lacking any kind of attraction, have been worshipped. The current theory that the things which have become the objects of a cult are those that have most forcibly impressed the mind of man is contradicted by history. The incomparable value attributed to such objects has nothing to do with their intrinsic character.

There is no active faith, however secular, that has not its fetishes where the same striking disproportion can be observed. A flag is only a bit of cloth; nevertheless a soldier will die to save it. Morality is no less rich in contrasts of this sort. Between a man and an animal the differences from the point of view of anatomy, physiology and psychology are only differences of degree, and yet man has a high moral dignity and an animal none. From the point of view of values they are separated by an abyss. Men are unequal in physical strength and in talent, and yet we tend to regard all as having equal moral value. No doubt moral equality is an ideal never to be realized, but we are drawing constantly nearer its realization. A postage stamp is a thin square of paper, lacking for the most part all artistic character, and yet it may be worth a fortune. Obviously it is not the intrinsic nature of pearls, diamonds, furs or laces that make the value of these different articles of dress vary at the caprice of fashion.

2

If value is not in the thing, not inherent in some characteristic of the empirical reality, does it follow that the source of value lies beyond experience and the empirically verifiable? This, in fact, is a theory maintained more or less explicitly by a line of thinkers whose doctrine derives *via* Ritschl from Kantian morality. They have supposed in man a *sui generis* faculty for transcending experience and for conceiving an extra-empirical reality—in a word, the ability to create ideals. This faculty of representation has been conceived in a more or less intellectual form by some and in a sentimental form by others, but always as quite distinct from the faculty exercised in scientific thought. Thus there is one way of considering the real and another, quite different, of considering the ideal. It is from the relation between reality and these ideals that values are estimated. Things are said to have value when they express or reflect, in any way whatsoever, an aspect of the ideal and to have more or less value according to the ideal and according to the degree to which they embody it.

Thus while in the preceding theories value judgments were offered as another form of judgments of reality, here the heterogeneity of the two is radical. The objects to which they refer are as distinct as the faculties they presuppose. The objections that we made to the first explanations will not apply to the second. It is easy to understand that the value and the nature of an object may to a certain extent be distinct and independent if the value is dependent upon causes exterior to the object. Further, the privileged place always given to the value of luxury is easily justified, since the ideal is not subordinate to the real; it exists for itself and therefore will not be measured by the interests of reality.

However, the value thus attributed to the ideal, while it explains much, does not explain itself. It is postulated but it is not, nor can it be, accounted for. If the ideal does not depend upon the real it would be impossible to find in the real the conditions and causes which would make it intelligible. But beyond the real where can the material for a satisfactory explanation be found? There is, in fact, something profoundly empiricist in this kind of idealism. It is a fact that men love a goodness, beauty and truth that are never adequately realized in action. But that itself is a fact unjustifiably exalted as a sort of absolute, beyond which we are forbidden to go. Further, we should wish to know how it comes about that we have both the need and the means for surpassing the real and imposing upon the world of matter a different world which the best of us make our home.

To this question the theological hypothesis makes a sort of answer. It postulates the existence of the world of ideals as a supra-experimental, but none the less objective, reality from which our empirical reality derives and depends. Thus we are joined to the ideal as the source of our being. Quite apart from other difficulties raised by this explanation, once the ideal has been hypostatized in this way it has at the same time become immobile, and all means of explaining its infinite variability are lost to us. We know today that not only is the ideal different in different groups, but also that it *should* vary. The ideal of the Romans was not, and cannot be, ours, and the scale of values varies accordingly. These changes are not due to human blindness but are based in the nature of the facts. How may they be explained if the ideal is one unassailable reality? We should be forced to admit that the Divinity varies in space and in time, and how can this be explained? The changing condition of God could only be intelligible if He had to realize an ideal beyond Himself, and anyhow this merely shifts the problem but does not change it.

By what reasoning can the ideal be said to be beyond nature and science? It manifests itself in nature and surely, then, depends upon natural causes. In order that it may be more than a mere possibility for speculation it must be desired, and must therefore have a force capable of swaying our wills. Our wills alone can make it a living reality. Since this force must ultimately be translated in terms of muscular movement it cannot differ essentially from the other forces of the universe. Why should it not be possible to analyse it, to resolve it into its elements and find those causes that determine the synthesis from which it results? We already have instances in which it is possible to measure it. Each human group at each moment in its history has a respect of a certain intensity for human dignity. It is this sentiment, varying among different people and at different times, that is at the root of the moral ideal of contemporary societies. Now accordingly as it is more or less strong, the number of criminal assaults against the person will be low or high. In the same way the number of adulteries, divorces and separations expresses the relative force with which the conjugal ideal makes itself felt. No doubt these are clumsy devices, but what measurement of any physical force can

be more than an approximation? In fact, the relation of
the one to the other shows that there are only differences
of degree between them.

Furthermore there is an order of values that cannot be
separated from reality without losing all significance; these
are economic values. It is generally accepted that these
express and imply no faculty of the supra-experimental.
For this reason Kant refused to consider them as real
values; he preferred to reserve this term solely for facts of the
moral order.[1] This exclusion is unjustified. Certainly there
are different types of value, but they are all species of the
same genus. All correspond to an evaluation of things
even though evaluation be made from different points of
view. The progress that the theory of values has made of
late lies in the establishment of the generality and unity
of this notion. If, then, the various types of value are
related, and if certain of them are so closely bound to our
empirical existence, the others cannot be independent of
that existence.

3

To sum up; if the value of a thing cannot be, and has never
been, estimated except in relation to some conception of
the ideal, the latter needs explanation. To understand how
value judgments are possible it is not enough to postulate
a certain number of ideals. Their origins, the way in which
they are related to, yet transcend, experience, and the nature
of their objectivity must be accounted for.

Since ideals and their corresponding value systems vary
with various human groups, does this not suggest a collective origin for both? It is true that we have already disposed
of one sociological theory of value which seemed insufficient, but that was because it rested upon a misconception
of the real nature of society. There society was presented

---

[1] He says that things in the economic sphere have a price (*einen
Preis, einen Marktpreis*) not an intrinsic value (*einen inneren Werth*).
5th edition, Hartenstein, vol. vii, pp. 270 et seq. and p. 614.

as a system of organs and functions, maintaining itself against outside forces of destruction just like a physical organism whose entire life consists in appropriate reactions to external stimuli. Society is, however, more than this, for it is the centre of a moral life (*le foyer d'une vie morale*) of which the strength and independence have not always been fully recognized.

When individual minds are not isolated but enter into close relation with and work upon each other, from their synthesis arises a new kind of psychic life. It is clearly distinguished by its peculiar intensity from that led by the solitary individual. Sentiments born and developed in the group have a greater energy than purely individual sentiments. A man who experiences such sentiments feels himself dominated by outside forces that lead him and pervade his milieu. He feels himself in a world quite distinct from that of his own private existence. This is a world not only more intense but also qualitatively different. Following the collectivity, the individual forgets himself for the common end and his conduct is orientated in terms of a standard outside himself. At the same time, and owing to their theoretical nature, these forces are not easily controlled, canalized and adjusted to closely determined ends. They need to overflow for the sake of overflowing, as in play without any specific objective, at one time in the form of stupid destructive violence or, at another, of heroic folly. It is in a sense a luxurious activity since it is a very rich activity. For all these reasons this activity is qualitatively different from the everyday life of the individual, as is the superior from the inferior, the ideal from the real.

It is, in fact, at such moments of collective ferment that are born the great ideals upon which civilizations rest. The periods of creation or renewal occur when men for various reasons are led into a closer relationship with each other, when reunions and assemblies are most frequent, relationships better maintained and the exchange of ideas most active. Such was the great crisis of Christendom, the movement of collective enthusiasm which, in the twelfth and thirteenth centuries, bringing together in Paris the scholars of Europe, gave birth to Scholasticism. Such were the Reformation and Renaissance, the revolutionary epoch and the Socialist upheavals of the nineteenth century. At such moments this higher form of life is lived with such intensity and exclusiveness that it monopolizes all minds to the more or less complete exclusion of egoism and the commonplace. At such times the ideal tends to become one with the real, and for this reason men have the impression that the time is close when the ideal will in fact be realized and the Kingdom of God established on earth. This illusion can never last because the exaltation cannot maintain itself at such a pitch; it is too exhausting. Once the critical moment has passed, the social life relaxes, intellectual and emotional intercourse is subdued, and individuals fall back to their ordinary level. All that was said, done and thought during this period of fecund up-heaval survives only as a memory, a memory no doubt as glorious as the reality it recalls, but with which it is no longer at one. It exists as an idea or rather as a composition of ideas. Between what is felt and perceived and what is thought of in the form of ideals there is now a clear distinction. Nevertheless these ideals could not survive if they were not periodically revived. This revivification is the function of religious or secular feasts and ceremonies, all public addresses in churches or schools, plays and exhibitions—in a word, whatever draws men together into an intellectual and moral communion. These moments are, as it were, minor versions of the great creative move-ment. But these means have only a temporary effect. For a short time the ideal comes to life and approaches reality, but it soon becomes differentiated from it.

If man conceives ideals, and indeed cannot help conceiv-ing and becoming attached to them, it is because he is a social being. Society moves or forces the individual to rise above himself and gives him the means for achieving this.

Through the very awareness of itself society forces the individual to transcend himself and to participate in a higher form of life. A society cannot be constituted without creating ideals. These ideals are simply the ideas in terms of which society sees itself and exists at a culminating point in its development. To see society only as an organized body of vital functions is to diminish it, for this body has a soul which is the composition of collective ideals. Ideals are not abstractions, cold intellectual concepts lacking efficient power. They are essentially dynamic, for behind them are the powerful forces of the collective. They are collective forces—that is, natural but at the same time moral forces, comparable to the other forces of the universe. The ideal itself is a force of this nature and therefore subject to scientific investigation. The reason why the ideal can partake of reality is that it derives from it while transcending it. The elements that combine to form the ideal are part of reality, but they are combined in a new manner and the originality of the method of combination produces the originality of the synthesis itself. Left alone, the individual could never find in himself the material for such a construction. Relying upon his own powers, he could never have the inclination or the ability to surpass himself. His personal experience might enable him to distinguish ends already realized from those to be desired, but the ideal is not simply something which is lacking and desired. It is not simply a future goal to which man aspires; it has its own reality and nature. It is to be thought of rather as looming impersonally above the individual wills that it moves. If it were the product of the individual will, how could it be impersonal? If in answer to this question the impersonal reason of humanity is appealed to, the question is again only shifted and not resolved. This latter impersonality is scarcely different from the first and must itself be accounted for. If minds are at one to this degree, it is, surely, because they derive their homogeneity from a common source and, in fact, participate in a common reason.

In order to explain value judgments it is not necessary either to lose the concept of value by reducing them to judgments of reality or to relate them to some faculty or other by which man enters into relations with the transcendental world. Certainly value derives from the relation of things to different aspects of the ideal, but the ideal is not 'cloud cuckoo land'; it is *of* and *in* nature. It is subject to examination like the rest of the moral or physical universe. The intellect can no more exhaust the ideal than it can any other aspect of reality, but it can be applied in the hope of a progressive understanding without assigning in advance a limit to this indefinite progress. From this point of view we can the more easily understand that the nature and the value of a thing can be distinct. Collective ideals can only be manifested and become aware of themselves by being concretely realized in material objects that can be seen by all, understood by all, and represented to all minds. Drawings, symbols of all sorts, formulae, whether written or spoken, animate or inanimate objects, provide examples of such concrete realizations. No doubt it may occur that the characteristics of certain objects have a natural affinity with the ideal, and thus it may seem, wrongly, that their intrinsic characteristics are themselves the cause of the value attached to the whole. But the ideal can, and does, attach itself where it will. All sorts of contingent circumstances determine the manner of its embodiment, and the object once chosen, however commonplace, becomes unique. In this way a rag achieves sanctity and a scrap of paper may become extremely precious. Two beings may be essentially different or from certain points of view unequal, but if they embody the same ideal they appear equal. In such a situation the ideal appears to be their most important common characteristic and overshadows their dissimilarities. In this way collective thought changes everything that it touches. It throws down the barriers of the realms of nature and combines contraries; it reverses what is called the natural hierarchy of being, makes disparity equal, and differentiates the similar. In a word, society substitutes for the world revealed to us by our senses a different world that is the projection of the ideals created by society itself.

4

What finally is the relation between value judgments and judgments of reality?

From the foregoing we have seen that there is no difference in nature. A value judgment expresses the relation of a thing to an ideal. The ideal is, like the thing, a given reality itself although of different order. The relation expressed unites two given terms as in a judgment of reality. No distinction arises here because of the bringing into play of ideals, for this is, in fact, common to both kinds of judgment. Concepts are equally constructions of the mind, and consequently ideals. It would not be difficult to demonstrate that these concepts are collective ideals, since concepts are formed in and through language, which is a collective thing. The elements of judgment are then the same on both sides. This is not to say that they can be reduced to each other; they are similar because they are the products of the same faculty. There is not one way of thinking and judging for dealing with existence and another for estimating value. All judgment is necessarily based upon given fact; even judgments of the future are related materially to the present or to the past. On the other hand, all judgment brings ideals into play. There cannot then be more than one faculty of judgment.

We have, nevertheless, indicated a difference that still persists. If all judgments involve ideals we have different species of ideals. The function of some is to express the reality to which they adhere. These are properly called concepts. The function of others is, on the contrary, to transfigure the realities to which they relate, and these are the ideals of value. In the first instance the ideal is a symbol of a thing and makes it an object of understanding.

In the second the thing itself symbolizes the ideal and acts as the medium through which the ideal becomes capable of being understood. Naturally the judgments vary according to the ideals involved. Judgments of the first order are limited to the faithful analysis and representation of reality, while those of the second order express that novel aspect of the object with which it is endowed by the ideal. This aspect is itself real, but not real in the same way that the inherent properties of the object are real. An object may lose its value or gain a different one without changing its nature; only the ideal need change. A value judgment, then, adds to the given fact in a sense, even though what is added has been borrowed from another fact of a different order. Thus the faculty of judgment functions differently according to the circumstances, but these differences do not impair the essential unity of the function.

Positive sociology has been accused of having a fetish for fact and a systematic indifference to the ideal. We can see now the injustice of such an accusation. The principal social phenomena, religion, morality, law, economics and aesthetics, are nothing more than systems of values and hence of ideals. Sociology moves from the beginning in the field of ideals—that is its starting-point and not the gradually attained end of its researches. The ideal is in fact its peculiar field of study. But (and here the qualification 'positive' is perhaps justified if such an adjective were not otiose before the word 'science') sociology cannot deal with the ideal except as a science. It does not set out to construct ideals, but on the contrary accepts them as given facts, as objects of study, and it tries to analyse and explain them. In the faculty of ideation (*faculté d'idéal*), sociology sees a natural faculty for which conditions and causes can be found for the purpose, if possible, of giving man a greater control of it. The aim is to bring the ideal, in its various forms, into the sphere of nature, with its distinctive attributes unimpaired. If to us, as sociologists, the task does not seem impossible, it is because society itself fulfils all the necessary conditions for presenting an account of these opposing characteristics. Society is also of nature and yet dominates it. Not only do all the forces of the universe converge in society, but they also form a new synthesis which surpasses in richness, complexity and power of action all that went to form it. In a word, society is nature arrived at a higher point in its development, concentrating all its energies to surpass, as it were, itself.